J. K. LASSER'S
FINANCIAL
PLANNING
FOR YOUR FAMILY

By The J. K. Lasser
Tax Institute

CORNERSTONE LIBRARY
NEW YORK

Reprinted 1980

Published by Cornerstone Library, Inc.
A Simon & Schuster Division of
Gulf & Western Corporation
Simon & Schuster Building
1230 Avenue of the Americas
New York, New York 10020

CORNERSTONE LIBRARY and colophon are trademarks
of Simon & Schuster, registered in the U.S. Patent and
Trademark Office.

Manufactured in the United States of America

ISBN 0-346-12410-7

Preface

The national economy is afflicted by inflation and energy shortages and threatened by recession. Inflation erodes buying power; the energy shortage raises costs and curtails production; recession could bring high unemployment and lower living standards. Personally we cannot solve these problems. But whatever economic condition prevails, we can try to protect ourselves and our families. For this purpose, J. K. LASSER'S GUIDE TO FINANCIAL PLANNING has been written for those who want to develop and follow an intelligent approach to family finances.

Whether you are single, without or with dependents, newly married, already established with a family, or on the way to retirement, you will find methods, advice, and suggestions for managing your personal finances. Read the book, check points of personal relevancy and then begin to use its suggestions systematically in the development of a personalized budget and financial program.

Your application of the ideas presented in this book can enable you to resolve many present financial difficulties and perhaps anticipate and solve future financial problems.

We gratefully acknowledge here the contributions of Barbara Weltman, Henrietta Danson and Katherine Torak.

Table of Contents

Using Credit Wisely

Buying Your Own Home or Condominium

CHAPTER 5

Your Investment Programs

CHAPTER 6

Your Life Insurance Program

CHAPTER 7
Planning Ahead for Retirement

CHAPTER 8
Keeping Records to Reduce Taxes

CHAPTER 1

Your Financial Program

Developing a Financial Program

A disciplined financial program can be used to advantage by everyone, in good times as well as bad. To the financially hard-pressed, it is essential; to the currently affluent person, it may act as a brake on a tendency to spend as if there is no tomorrow. Tomorrow may dawn bleakly. Moreover, planning for a secure financial future cannot be postponed. The young should consider it; the middle-aged must consider it; the elderly reap the results of planning or lack of it.

In the following pages, you will find how to assess net worth, budget, achieve goals, and establish financial security. Such basic planning can be adapted by young career people, those newly married and people of all ages who constantly run into financial problems.

When young marrieds set up a plan, they will, of course, change their pattern if a working wife stops working; when they start a family; and if they move from an apartment to a house. They will budget afresh with each change, enlarging their system, and redirecting saving toward new goals. Through frank discussion and planning together, a couple can build an invaluable bulwark against future inharmony.

The single person who has no present plans for marriage, or to set up housekeeping with another, may still have to budget carefully to achieve financial goals. Some singles have children to bring up, some have responsibilities toward a parent, some have educational debts to repay. A single needs a budget no less than a couple. Let wrangling over past mistakes go. Make a decision to work together to overcome difficulties and to build a more satisfying life through the wiser use of money.

Children should not be left out of financial planning. Their future is involved too. Seek their interest and cooperation early; you will find it a sound investment.

The Budget

Smart financial management starts with a budget, or, if you prefer another name, a money allocation plan. In the home, in personal life, as well as in business, the budget is a means of controlling expenses and of directing spending wisely. Many people recoil at the very idea. They think a budget is a strait jacket - something that will tie them down and take all the joy out of living. On the contrary, the budget is a means of releasing money to better use and of putting the budgeter in control of his fortunes. It is a way out of continued financial harassment, and a tool with which to handle rising costs, taxation, sudden sickness, and other emergencies. It means money at work for you, achieving your objectives, present and future.

Programming Income

The following budget plan covers two classes of people: Those who earn regular salaries or wages (with or without other sources of income), and those whose income is uncertain and irregular.

While the experienced budgeter usually plans ahead for a calendar year (the period we will illustrate), the new budgeter may prefer to set up a shorter program. If you wish, start with a three-month trial period. You can enlarge it later.

You may find it helpful to do rough planning on large sheets of paper that will not restrict you. Use unglazed shelf paper if you like, or tape sheets together. Later, when you have decided on your personal setup, you can transfer to a suitable columnar book or pages, or rule up a large notebook.

It is a good idea to pencil in projected figures so you can conform or change them later. If you use ink or ball point for a whole period, you are likely to end up with confusion, or else feel you have an inflexible chart that is going to tie you down.

Step I—The Pattern of Your Income

If you are steadily employed, you can probably forecast your income for the year. You also know what additional sources you usually have, such as savings bank interest, dividends, regular gifts, bonuses, and income from rentals, profitable hobbies, part-time work, etc.

Draw up your Step I form into fifteen columns as indicated below:

Source of Cash Funds	Jan.	Feb.	Mar.	(etc. . . . . . . .Dec.)									Total	Notes
Take-home pay:														
Husband														
Wife														
Interest														
Dividends														
Other														
Total														

Project your figures across the year (or shorter period). If you expect a raise, change the entries *after* you have it. A smart policy in money management is never to spend such money in advance or even to plan on covering essentials with it. Many people get in trouble with credit payments because the money they counted on failed to come through. You play safe when you work on a minimum basis.

If you are employed, your company does part of your budgeting before you receive your pay check. Amounts listed on an accompanying slip advise you of the deductions made for such items as federal, state, and city taxes, Social Security (FICA), state disability insurance, health insurance, pension fund. Those last four items can be termed assets rather than liabilities, since you have protection and possible financial return from them.

If you are self-employed, you must set aside funds to meet the above types of commitment yourself. Taxes must be estimated and paid quarterly; you are responsible for social security payments; you need health insurance; without a company pension plan, you will want to set aside the amount allowed for an Individual Retirement Account (IRA).

You may estimate savings bank interest and dividends. You might pencil in last year's figures as a guide. (If you never draw on interest, dividends, or other income for living expenses, but maintain these amounts in your savings and investment program, you will, of course, omit the figures from a budget.) Meeting all financial commitments from take-home pay will help you save for such long-term goals as home ownership, a new car, vacations, and educational expenses.

If your employment is irregular, or depends on business profits or commissions, you will probably have to use last year's figures or a reasonable estimate in your projection. The person who receives income in large amounts at irregular intervals is often prone to spending sprees, then has to borrow to meet the inevitable bills. If you are in this category, start now with discipline; be conservative in your plans, basing them on minimum expectations. You may find it helpful to total expected income for the year, divide it by 12, and to allow yourself only one-twelfth for each month. You are then on the same basis as the regular wage and salary earner, but because your total is uncertain till received, you should exercise restraint in spending until you have directed savings into a solid bank account.

Finish up your Step I form now with a line of monthly totals.

Step II—Programming Your Commitments

Draw up a 15-column form similar to that used in Step I.

Fixed Expenses	(January through December)	Total	Notes
Total			

On the left under the main heading of Fixed Expenses, note down this type of obligation:

Additional Federal, state, and city taxes

Mortgage or rent

Repayments of all types of loans and installment purchases

Insurance premiums

Telephone, heat, light, water, etc.

Pledged contributions

Society or union dues

Savings (a fixed obligation for single or married) for future goals and emergencies.

You know when these fixed expenses have to be paid. Some are certain in amount and you can project them across twelve months. Some are variable, such as the telephone bill. You can use previous bills or estimate this type of upcoming payment.

Note that Step II does not include department store and similar billing, only installment payments, if any. This step is designed to cover your fixed expenses of which regular savings should be a part.

Summarizing Steps I and II, Adjustments

You now have a total line for your income (Step I), and one for your fixed expenses (Step II). In summarizing, you can use a separate paper if you prefer, but if you have room, save copying by running your Step II totals under those of Step I. Deduct one from the other. The resulting figure shows what you now have available for your everyday expenses.

	(January through December)												Total
Step I (Total Income)													
Step II (Fixed Expenses)													
Available for													
Step III (Everyday expenses)													

No doubt your Step III line is uneven because you have more heavy expenses one month than another. Perhaps the expenses of some months will be so heavy you are practically in the red for your everyday expenditures. You also see some months show few, if any, fixed expenses.

Here are ways to make an adjustment:

Some people make a total of the heavy obligations that only come up about once or twice a year, divide the total by twelve, and bank that sum monthly. By so averaging, they prepare for vacations, certain taxes, insurance premiums, and educational expenses.

Total cost

Taxes $

Insurance

Heating

Vacation

Education   _____

Total   ÷ 12 = (amount to be set aside monthly)

On the other hand, you may want to consider each item separately in order to project the figures across the budget form.

People with few fixed expenses may prefer to even up their adjustment form simply by raising the savings on Step II so that Step III comes out to a more or less even monthly figure.

Exactly how the juggling and adjusting is done is your personal affair. *The aim is to arrive at a consistent monthly figure for everyday expenses in line with the budget you draw up in Step III.* As you can see, it will be necessary for you to work backwards and forwards on these steps before you can develop the best plan through which you can reach the objectives you have named.

Throughout your early budget experiments, remind yourself that you will need at least a full year of record keeping before you can come up with reasonably settled forms and figures. When people read of budget plans, they often assume they can solve their financial difficulties overnight by just filling in the suggested forms. Usually, a personal situation is far too complex for such an easy solution. Certainly it is in the case of a family. *The budget works for you - when you have worked at it.*

Step III—The Key to Your Budget

A period of recording your present rate of expenditure is necessary before you can settle on the most profitable plan for everyday expenses. Only by seeing how much you are presently spending in certain categories can you set up an improved pattern.

Both marrieds and singles will have to set up many aspects of the budget on a tentative and experimental basis, but keeping track of all spending will provide invaluable records. Though it may be annoying to keep noting down all amounts spent, it is absolutely necessary to good money management to find out exactly where the money is going.

Some budgeters, once in the habit of such record keeping, prefer to continue it. Most people find it too constricting and, once they have established a suitable set-aside for a particular category, such as food, will not continue to run the last dime to earth. Plan on at least two months of strict record keeping in which all members of a family participate, and note that if you keep these records in summer your pattern may be different in winter. A budget readjustment may be called for seasonally within the set figure you arrive at for Step III.

The Categories of Everyday Expenditure

Base daily accounting on the headings you intend to use when making up your budget. Following is a list of suggested main categories and the types of expenditure which would be entered under each:

Food. In this category, include food bought for meals at home, school lunches, and all meals out. Alcoholic and soft drinks and candy should be included, also any taxes and tips.

Household Maintenance. Repairs, supplies, paid help or services.

Furnishings and Equipment. This will cover furniture, floor coverings, accessories such as tableware, curtains, and slipcovers, television, radios, etc., cleaning of any items.

Clothing. Dry cleaning, laundry, and charges by tailor and dressmaker would come under this heading as well as garments and the material for making them.

Transportation. Automobile upkeep and operation; commutation expenses, air, train, bus, and taxi fares.

Health Care. Fees for professional services, including hospital, drugs, supplies, and eyeglasses.

Education. Textbooks, supplies, tuition.

Recreation. Entertainment, reading, hobby material, games.

Personal Care. Beauty parlor and barber's charges, toilet items, etc.

Family Allowances. Each person's spending money.

In general, avoid overanalysis. It can prove tiresome and discouraging unless it serves a particular aim. So, separate details only when necessary. The cost of meals out can go in with other food unless you are reporting them as business expenses or you need to track down where the food dollars are going.

Of course, you will need details and receipts of items you may be deducting for income tax, or need to record for inventory or insurance purposes. Too, you may wish to separate cash from check transactions.

Methods of Keeping Track

We suggest spending be noted in a small book or pad carried in purse or pocket. Receipts and store tapes should be placed in a prearranged place in the home, such as a box, a drawer, or on a spindle. Enter these outgoing payments on a form drawn up in accordance with your personal or family situation and need of specific details.

Here is a suggestion:

Date	Food		Clothing		Housing			Transportation		Health		Personal		Etc.
	At home	Out	Pur-chases	Cleaning Repairs	Phone	Supplies	Furnish-ings	Car	Other	Doctor Drugs	Den-tist	Allow-ance, hair care	Drinks tobacco candy	
Total														

Work out a full form according to your own type of expenses, the number of people in the family, and the need to subdivide (which should not be carried to excess). Note the points on which the suggestion above differs from the list. For example, these headings show the telephone under everyday expenses. Earlier, we showed it on Step II as a fixed expense. You can place it as it best suits you, or split the set rental charge from excess charges, especially if you wish to place a limit on family calls.

Since this record-keeping is to account for everyday expenses, we omit the Step II (page 15) items, such as rent, insurance, utilities. Nevertheless, you may well want to record them separately so that at the end of a month you can accurately show:

Total income for January   _____

Total expenditure for the month   _____

(Cash in hand to meet a saving or
   spending goal)   _____

Weighing Up Your Spending

If you are fortunately not overspending, you now only have to keep on the same track, perhaps making a few adjustments within certain categories. If, even better, you can draw a line under income less expenses for the month above and show a saving, you have money in hand to put in the bank or to satisfy needs on your list of goals.

Many people find themselves overspent, using money they should have put into savings or have gone to the bank and taken out money already saved or, worse still, they have borrowed to cover expenses. If you are overspent, trim spending for next month. Do not take on more fixed expenses (Step II), such as installment payments. Let the spending goals wait until you have a surplus. Be patient with your record-keeping and planning. You may have to allocate more to clothes, for example, when children need outfitting for school; plans for household purchases must temporarily be shelved. The experienced budgeter learns how to rob Peter to pay Paul; but he or she keeps within the total allocated for the flexible expenses for that period.

Your Step III Budget Form

After you have been keeping records for a period, you can project figures on an annual basis (though you may not find it practical to plan closely for more than two or three months in advance). Below, a form is suggested:

Through this form you control your budget because, if you keep spending in line with projections here, you are fulfilling your other objectives, covering the Step II fixed expenses, and the savings program.

	Jan	Feb	Mar	Apr	May	Jun	Jul	Aug	Sep	Oct	Nov	Dec	Notes
Food													
Housing													
Clothes													
etc.													
etc.													
Total													

If you set up a record of what you actually spent and compare it with your plan, you will have a useful guide to help you to cut back - and to maintain a vital reserve fund.

At times, of course, your control over Step III expenditures may break down. Unexpected medical bills may roll in, just at the same time you have to pay the plumber, painter, and roofer or the rent goes up when you can least afford the extra payment. *The only sound answer to such emergencies is the reserve in your savings account.*

Until you have that reserve in a substantial condition, set a minimum operational figure for your everyday expenditure, and make the necessary adjustments within that figure. Members of a family group and individuals must establish what is essential and what is not. Tough times mean tough decisions. Cut down on spending so that the reserve can be stepped up.

As we have noted, it may not be practical to budget daily expenditure for more than two months in advance, and sometimes a shorter period is desirable. But when your Step III form is fully developed, you should have established a reasonable sum which, each month, will cover daily needs and take care of the bills. In today's economy, you have to be ready to spend more for food. housing, repairs, etc. At times, a budget must be flexible - as when an outlay at sales may represent a substantial saving. Using a budget rather than letting it use you is an art you can acquire. Unless you are heavily in debt, you need never develop any sense that a budget is a limiting factor in your life.

Upcoming Variable Bills

A hurdle which frequently throws the hopeful new budgeter is the charge account. Weeks after the purchases are made, the bills arrive. If provision has not been made for their payment, interest charges may be incurred on the accounts.

You should keep a record of credit spending so that you will be ready for the billing. Note the date each department store or other company usually bills you; if one company bills on the sixth of the month and another on the sixteenth and you are paid twice a month you can set aside the money in your checking account from two pay checks.

If you are already working your budget you will be less haphazard in your buying than formerly, and not buying in excess of planned items. But because people do tend to buy on sight (and sometimes it may be wise to do so), a record of what is being charged (from gasoline to garden tools) will help in adjusting next month's plan to meet the expected bills.

The Deduction Method Of Keeping Track

Once people kept their budgeted money in cash, in envelopes or jars. These days money allocated to a certain category may be in cash, a checking account, and a savings account. How can you keep track of your spending?

An idea you may find useful is to set up index cards or pages of a notebook which show the budgeted amount in each category and then to deduct from it as purchases are made. For example, the mother of a family knows the agreed sum for clothing buying this month. She has cash in hand for small purchases, the rest in checking and savings accounts. Carrying a card in her purse, she marks down charged shoes and a dress; her husband reports at night his cash purchase of shirts; a teenage daughter who has been handed cash returns the change and reports the buying of a skirt. Deductions from the budgeted amount show only a few dollars left. The family can readily see that, except for minor purchases, clothing buying is over for the budgeting period.

A variation of this method is to give each member of the family cards with his portion of the budgeted category on it.

Some budgeters can carry their budget in their heads, but when several members of the family are spending, the deduction method can help to solve problems in money management.

Use Savings Accounts in Budget Plans

Passbook savings accounts at local banks and thrift institutions are valuable tools for the budgeter. As suggested earlier, one account can be used for "fixed" expense bills; then keep a book record showing how much you are setting aside in each category.

Long-term projects can be accomplished in much the same way.

Your regular savings. Savings have been listed in your budget plan as a definite commitment to be handled as regularly and seriously as paying the taxman. Assume husband and wife earn, and agree on saving $400 a month from their combined salaries. Savings objectives include such items as emergency fund, vacation, gifts, starting a family, down payment on a house, investments, education costs, retirement, home imporvements, furniture, major appliances. Some are long-term, some short-term goals. The couple might choose to place $50 a month to build up an emergency fund if they do not already have the equivalent of about six-months earnings in hand; $100 a month might be needed for a period to cover upcoming higher education costs for one or the other; $100 a month goes into a down payment fund as the couple looks ahead from apartment renting to home ownership; an interest-paying Christmas or Chanukah club can be used for holiday season gift buying; other regular savings are allocated for medical care, travel, major items of clothing, and investments, an item fully discussed below.

How the Budgeter Uses Credit

It might appear from the foregoing that budgeters pay cash and do not use credit cards. But, of course, establishing a sound credit record is necessary in today's society so a budgeting family will certainly make use of oil company, bank, department store, and club credit cards as needed. The trick of using credit when budgeting is not to sign for more than you could, in fact, pay in cash. The wise budgeter does not run credit interest charges but may let his funds accumulate interest in a savings account until payment on bills is due.

As an example of using credit, take the purchase of clothing for which individuals or family allow a specified amount in everyday or flexible expenses, and also save regularly. The saved funds are best used at sale time when high-priced items such as winter coats, men's suits, and footwear should be bought. The amount of cash accumulated in the clothing account is noted and not exceeded when the purchases are made and charged. The sum allocated in cash to clothing will be needed for cleaning, repairs, and minor or low-priced purchases.

Budgeting for Investments

Investments in stocks, mutual funds, Treasury notes and bills, and business ventures are discussed in later chapters. But the first step for many individuals and families will be the building up of savings which can eventually be channelled into high-return, possibly tax-exempt, investments for which minimum initial payments are necessary. While savings in banks and thrift institutions enjoy insurance protection, the same is not true of many other forms of investment. Therefore, the budgeter will not want to venture into possible areas of risk or tying up of funds before there is a substantial cushion of funds for emergencies and for family needs.

Handling a Debt Problem

You may have come to budgeting because of a debt problem. The extended use of credit has landed many individuals and families in trouble—high-income people as well as those in modest circumstances. The debt-burdened not only have to learn to budget to meet present and future expenses, they must also rid themselves of the problem by the same means.

If bills are not too large, and the creditors are persuadable, you can probably work out a regular plan of payment from each pay check. If creditors know that a debtor is ready to handle repayment systematically, they are more likely to sit down and help work out a plan.

Where debts are too heavy, the creditors applying pressure, and it seems impossible to handle repayment from income, there may be no alternative but a "rehabilitation" loan. By getting a loan, the debtor can settle quickly, but of course the loan must be repaid with interest. A number of banks and also reputable small loan companies offer counseling as well as refinancing; they will work with the debtor in setting up a debt-repayment plan.

Before getting a rehabilitation loan, debtors should seek advice from a reliable source. Clergymen are usually in a position to channel people to suitable advisors. Community and family services may offer counsel. Some cities have specific advice centers for the indebted. A consumer credit-counseling service, a nonprofit organization, may be contacted. If a call to "city hall" does not provide a lead, a local bank manager may be able to point the way. The last thing a debtor needs is to fall into the hands of a loan shark—and it can happen to people who are too upset and frightened to get qualified credit counseling.

Family Cooperation in Budgeting

In putting forward suggestions for your financial program we have assumed that husband, wife, and family have come to terms, can discuss the situation frankly and can make reasonable, harmonious plans for earning and spending.

This is the ideal situation, but it must be recognized that some families face areas of violent conflict over money. Psychological difficulties may lead to gambling, wildcat investments, or lavish generosity out of all keeping with circumstances. A husband or wife may be a spendthrift or a penny pincher; one may indulge in needless spending even after agreeing to a plan to pay off debts; another cuts corners and subjects the family to financial squeezing and unwarranted limitation. Such people may well be among those who must eventually have professional advice.

This is a book on money management, not psychological counsel. Where this type of help is necessary it may be found through a Family Service Agency, which can be located through a telephone directory. Where none can be traced, write to Family Service Association of America, 44 East 23rd Street, New York, New York 10010 for names and addresses of agencies in your area.

Work together on the spending plan. One of the first decisions to be reached in a family money management program is—who will manage what. If you are only just married, you have a good chance to come to an early understanding on this subject—and so to avoid one of the conflicts that endanger marriage. If you are long-married and the division of responsibility is a source of trouble, decide now to start afresh. The following steps outline a reasonable program:

Begin with a working partnership in handling money. In cases where the husband is the sole wage-earner, the paycheck he receives is not his alone, to be doled out as he pleases. His wife earns her share, and often works a far longer day in the home. Here, we are concerned with the husband's salary which should be used to cover all major expenses for the family. Responsibility for its distribution belongs to both partners. From a joint checking account, the husband might handle items such as rent or mortgage, taxes, insurance, and expenses of the family automobile. From the same account, the wife could take over food and clothing expenses, probably the utility bills, and the cost of entertaining at home. List the type of bills faced in your household and decide which items husband or wife will handle. Often the wife will look after budgeting and keep the records of expenditures. Much depends on personal temperment and ability. Sometimes one partner is poor at figures and has no money sense at all. When both husband and wife lack wisdom in buying, the marriage can be headed for debt and trouble. Outside family counsel is invariably needed.

Establish working habits. Help yourself in the job of budgeting and paying bills by setting up a special area in the home where papers are to be kept. If all members of the household know that a certain drawer or portion of a desk is for bills, financial records, checkbooks, etc., there is little possibility of payments being overlooked. Establish your own "in and out" system of bills, from receipt in the mail to payment. File receipts carefully. You may need them at income tax time.

Whatever system you use, accompany it with a definite set-aside of time to enter figures in your own records and to write checks. If you fail to establish a regular schedule for dealing with your plans, payments, and records, the good management of money is unlikely to happen for you!

Establishing Your Net Worth

No financial program can be made for the future without finding out where you stand today, and annually thereafter.

Turn to the forms given below. They will help you make your tabulations. Add and delete headings to suit yourself, but see that you cover all items that add to your total worth and every liability against it.

ANNUAL FINANCIAL STATEMENT

(Date)

ASSETS

Cash on hand	$_____
Checking accounts	_____
Savings accounts	_____
Money lent to others (repayment expected)	_____
Value of life insurance (cash surrender value plus dividend accumulations)	_____
Annuities	_____
Retirement funds	_____
U.S. Savings bonds	_____
Investments -	_____
Stocks, bonds, mutual fund shares	_____
Real estate	_____
Pension and profit-sharing plans	_____
Your home - full market value	_____
Other property (list such items as)	_____
Automobile	_____
Household furnishings	_____
Furs, jewelry	_____
Sports and hobby items	_____
Clothing, etc.	_____
Total Assets	$_____

ANNUAL FINANCIAL STATEMENT

(Date)

LIABILITIES

Unpaid Bills	$_____
Charge accounts	_____
Credit card accounts	_____
Taxes	_____
Insurance premiums	_____
Other	_____
Balances Due on-	_____
Installment contracts	_____
Loans (from banks, savings and loan	_____
associations, insurance companies,	
etc.)	
Other	_____
Mortgages payable on home and other	
property (or rent)	_____
Total Liabilities	$_____

SUMMARY

Assets	$_____
Liabilities	_____
Net Worth	$_____

In completing your statement, you may need to ask your insurance agent, your employer, and your bank for help in filling in figures on annuities, retirement funds, and U.S. Savings Bonds.

Be objective when you value such property as home, automobile, household equipment, personal items. What would they bring on the market today? For example, has your neighborhood appreciated or depreciated? Your local newspaper's real estate section is a useful source of information for property prices. An automobile dealer's Blue Book will help you make a realistic estimate of your car's worth. Personal property is hard to value. How much would you get if you were putting it up for sale? Clothing and equipment may depreciate, but antiques, paintings, and hobby collections could acquire value. Custom mart advertising and the columns of specialty journals at the library may help in making an assessment.

Use today's quotations to get the value of stocks, bonds, mutual shares. Disregard any gains or losses that may occur later.

With your net worth established, you and your family can plan for the year. You are in a position to make a five-year plan, as business and governments do, and can gear income and expenses to the fulfillment of your objectives. Note, too, that net worth data is essential to planning for retirement and for your estate.

Your Family Records

Calculating your net worth has necessitated your referring to many personal papers. Because many people need to organize in this important area, we discuss it below.

Do you know where all your important family records are now? Your marriage certificate, your will, Social Security card? Your employment record, listing employers, salary earned; your present standing in a profit-sharing or pension plan? And all the documents connected with your home, insurance, investment, or installment buying? If you know exactly where to find such data, you are more methodical and wiser than many of your neighbors. All too often, when emergencies arise, vital documents cannot be located. Sometimes they are misplaced through neglect or sheer carelessness; sometimes the one person who knows where the papers are is stricken by illness or accident. The problem can be avoided; see the suggested form of record keeping on the next page.

Your Net Worth and How It Changed for the Year

		PRESENT OR OPENING VALUE	CLOSING VALUE (IN 1 YEAR)	INCREASE OR DECREASE
YOU OWN	CASH			
	in checking account	$	$	$
	in savings accounts			
	INVESTMENTS (Market Value)			
	U.S. bonds			
	tax-free bonds			
	other bonds			
	stocks			
	mutual funds			
	REAL ESTATE (Market Value)			
	home			
	investment property			
	INSURANCE			
	cash surrender value plus dividend accumulations			
	OTHER PERSONAL PROPERTY (Market Value)			
	automobile			
	jewelry			
	other			
	loans to others (repayment expected)			
	pension and retirement funds			
	TOTAL YOU OWN	$	$	$
YOU OWE	**UNPAID CURRENT BILLS**	$	$	$
	charge accounts			
	credit card accounts			
	taxes			
	PERSONAL LOANS & INSTALLMENT DEBT			
	MORGAGE (balance)			
	OTHER LIABILITIES			
	TOTAL YOU OWE	$	$	$
	NET WORTH (Total owned less total owed)	$	$	$

Keep a Record Book

Family records will, of course, differ according to the assets owned, but the whereabouts of all data should be set down. If a loose-leaf notebook is used, it is easy to have extra photocopies made of all or any of the pages. It may be desirable for duplicate information to be in the hands of adult children, or kept at an office. Printed record books are obtainable, but you may prefer to make your own in line with your other financial records and inventories of valuables.

Here are some important items which should be listed with a note of reference about their location:

Certificates of birth; marriage; divorce; death; naturalization; and adoption papers. Official documents of life's major events are essential for innumerable purposes, to prove date and place of birth, to obtain American citizenship for the foreign-born, to claim Social Security benefits. If one or other of such important certificates is missing, obtain a certified copy in case it is needed - to collect on insurance, to claim an inheritance, to obtain a passport, or when remarriage takes place. You may not yet know of all the occasions when members of the family will need one or another of these major documents.

If you need a certified copy of a birth or death certificate, inquire at your state or city's central vital statistics office, usually associated with the Department of Health.

Social Security. Members of the family who have cards should make a note of the numbers and where the cards are usually kept. The cards come in two parts, so you may keep the stubs with other important records. Then, if a card is lost, a stub can be mailed to your local Social Security office with a request for a duplicate. Supply name, address, and place of business, in addition to the number, when writing.

Bank accounts. List bank names and addresses with the numbers of savings account books and the names of the members of the family who own each one. Each year banks advertise for missing depositors who have either forgotten their accounts or died without informing their relatives of them. See that the necessary information is available in your family.

Also list the names and addresses of banks where you and any others have checking accounts, and the numbers of those accounts.

United States savings bonds. Maintain a careful record of your bonds, noting full serial numbers, issue dates, and denomination. If the bonds themselves are lost, stolen, or destroyed, send such information at once to the Bureau of the Public Dept., Division of Loans and Currency, 536 South Clark Street, Chicago, Illinois 60605. You will then receive full information on how to get replacements.

Insurance of all types. Record information about each policy, its number, amount payable, and method of settlement. Include information about any personal coverage at place of business, such as participation in group health, pension, or profit-sharing benefits. List names and addresses of all companies involved and state where policies are kept.

Credit cards. Legislation and protective measures taken by issuers of credit cards have cut down on the responsibility of holders for goods and services charges by thieves. Nevertheless, you should list all your account numbers and the names and addresses of the issuing company. Advise loss immediately by phone or wire, and confirm in writing.

Inventory. It has already been suggested that you keep a household inventory in a bank safe deposit box. If you do not have one, use a fireproof box at home. If you file at the bank, you might want a duplicate of your inventory in your record book, so you can see when additions and reappraisals are necessary on the original.

Your Safe Deposit Box

For a small sum a safe deposit box can be rented at your bank. Here, you can safeguard valuable jewelry, stock certificates, deeds, legal records of all types, passports, bankbooks, personal papers, and the above mentioned inventory. Your will is best left with your attorney, but a copy should go in the box.

You will have to guard the keys to the box, for you are the sole possessor and you should appoint a deputy who can open the box in case you cannot. Check with the bank on its regulations affecting deputies.

You might also discuss with your attorney the legal implications which might arise, particularly at time of death, if you rent the safe deposit box jointly with your spouse.

Your Agenda and Its Priorities

You now have before you an assessment of your net worth. It will serve as a guide to what is financially possible for you and the family as you together establish an agenda. The objectives on that agenda, and those you name as priorities will, of course, reflect your circumstances and what now seems most important to achieve. If you are young, perhaps living in an apartment, home ownership may be the initial goal, together with a sound insurance program. Later, planning for your children's education may be the prior aim. Ultimately, you will be looking toward retirement.

In between come many types of long- and short-term priorities from new furnishings to vacation travel, automobiles and television, or perhaps dealing with sudden but temporary adversity, such as a job loss, accident, or sickness in the family.

Whatever your targets are, write them down, and then define *exactly how you will finance them*. Out of current income, from the savings, insurance, and investment program? Tie your objectives into your savings funds. Some may come within a one-year program. But as you set up those one-year projects, do not fail to look five years ahead. Will you then have increased education expenses? Or a likely commitment to an elderly member of the family?

Think your objectives through, and do not let too many short-term goals absorb your savings while you fail to take note of middle and long range needs. Plot out the five-and ten-year objectives so that, in due time, you are making provision toward retirement. Such planning for many people begins in middle life when they purchase a summer home and so locate a second community where they can establish roots in readiness for full-time residence in later years.

You are planning now with finances as they actually are. If certain objectives seen impossible because of limited means, weigh the budget and decide if some areas could stand trimming. It might be added that if money management is to be really sound, it needs to be well seasoned with humor and a certain element of relaxation. The people who frowningly deny themselves and their family a minor joy because "it is not in the budget," and the people who cheerfully dump every resolution for a spending spree need to work toward middle ground. As you set up your program, see it is built there.

CHAPTER 2

How and Where To Save Your Money

Do you get more for your money at a particular bank or thrift institution when you open a savings account? At this writing, the difference in types of service offered by commercial banks, mutual savings banks, and savings and loan associations is diminishing, and may be further lessened by changes in regulations. It is important to compare the savings opportunities offered by these financial institutions, and to consider a credit union too, if you are eligible to join one. In addition, there are such safe alternatives as U.S. savings bonds, Treasury notes, bills, and bonds, and other securities of the government.

In this chapter, we offer guidance so that you may make the most profitable and businesslike choice possible for the needs of yourself and your family.

Types of Financial Institution

Commercial banks. You may need a commercial bank for services not offered by thrift institutions in your area; indeed, in some communities, a commercial bank may be the only place offering savings accounts; there is no local competition. Maximum interest rates have, by law, been held 1/4 percent below the terms offered by the thrifts, but this regulation, long under fire, may vanish. Until recently, checking accounts were only opened at commercial banks and no interest was earned. Today, alternatives are spreading across the country, and in many areas interest-earning checking accounts are available under certain conditions at commercial banks and at thrift institutions.

Mutual savings banks. First established over 150 years ago, mutual savings banks operate in a limited number of states, mainly in the Northeast. These institutions have no stockholders, so, after payment of operating expenses, taxes, and additions to reserves, all earnings are paid to depositors as interest on savings. Chiefly, the business of these banks is to make loans.

Services today offered by mutual savings banks may include checking accounts, safe deposit boxes, Christmas and Chanukah clubs, sale of travelers' checks and United States savings bonds. Large mutuals may handle foreign remittances. In certain states, mutual savings banks sell low cost life insurance.

A variety of savings accounts, regular, day-of-deposit to day-of-withdrawal, time, are offered at mutuals. A small bank may offer precisely the same return as a large bank for long-term accounts, but the deposit may be larger.

Most mutual savings banks offer free bank-by-mail service. For customers living where best interest rates are not available, and for those who do not get around freely, banking by mail can be a problem solver.

Savings and loan associations. Savings and loan or building and loan associations which first appeared here in 1831 are to be found in every state. As a savings depositor, you become a shareholder, one of a group that lends in return for interest. As with a mutual savings bank, you may be both depositor and borrower at your "S & L," since loans, particularly mortgages, are very much their business. S & L's are similar to mutual savings banks in some respects though their operating rules differ. Bank-by-mail service is usually available.

Depending on its size and location, a savings and loan association may offer such attractions as free money orders and travelers' checks.

Credit unions. These private organizations are a special type of institution for savings and loans, owned and operated by the members, usually persons in a closely knit group, such as teachers, employees of companies, and members of labor unions, fraternal or social lodges, etc. These cooperative credit societies encourage the members to save systematically and offer free life insurance and low-cost unsecured loans to shareholders.

Traditionally, membership in a credit union has been restricted to persons having a common bond. The bond could be a common occupation such as acting, or even residence within a well-defined neighborhood, community, or rural district; it could be membership in a church, society, farm organization. Or a credit union might be made up of residents in a natural trade area of a rural community or rural district. Now, feminists are among those forming groups and young people get together in student credit unions. Further expansion is to be expected.

The Safety of Your Savings

Wherever placed, be sure your savings have insurance protection. Funds placed in accounts at commercial banks and mutual savings banks are protected through the Federal Deposit Insurance Corporation (FDIC); the Federal Savings and Loan Insurance Corporation (FSLIC) guarantees safety for savings in savings and loan associations. In some states, savings are protected by state insurance agencies. At this time, $40,000 is the limit for payment to depositors in case of failure on the part of the savings institution; a higher figure may become effective because $40,000 is widely regarded as too low.

Although all the savings accounts an individual may have in a particular institution are not covered beyond the $40,000 limit, there are a substantial number of combinations a couple or family can arrange so that coverage of more than $40,000 is insured. Joint accounts, testamentary revocable trust accounts, and irrevocable trust accounts arranged with spouse and children mean that thousands of dollars can safely be kept at one savings institution. The alternative is, of course, to use a number of such institutions and not exceed $40,000 at each one.

Individual Retirement Accounts (IRAs) are separately insured up to $100,000.

Yield on Savings

Not all savings institutions offer maximum rates allowed under the law. This is particularly true in small towns and rural locations where there is little competition. But even large city commercial banks may lag behind; many customers are unaware their funds could earn more money elsewhere.

Compounding and crediting of interest. Banks and savings institutions differ widely in compounding, crediting, and paying interest. New customers may see the same rates advertised at several savings institutions, but only by specific inquiry can the saver find which will pay best. Government regulations call for banks to give new customers full information on interest computation and to advise any change of system later adopted. Make sure you get the details you want.

Sometimes, differences are not significant. For example, a financial institution might advertise continuous compounding of interest, a competitor daily compounding. On $1,000 at 5 percent the advantage is four cents a year. More important is the crediting of interest to the depositor's passbook; see that you secure quarterly crediting; monthly would be better; twice a year is insufficient.

Some banks pay interest only on the lowest balance in an account during an interest period. Others operate complicated systems of offsetting withdrawals against deposits in such a way as to deny the customer the full benefit of interest he thought the account was earning.

When Savings Are Withdrawn

Before opening a day-of-deposit to day-of-withdrawal or regular account, find out the rules on withdrawals. Is prior notice required? Are any service charges imposed if withdrawals exceed a prescribed number? Try to avoid the savings institution which imposes restrictions or penalties on withdrawals. With the advent of electronic fund transfer (EFT) systems, customers may find charges levied for the withdrawal of funds from a savings to a checking account; such charges may differ from one financial institution to another, and may not exist at all under another system. New developments. new regulations, new types of service are on the way, and customers have to ascertain for themselves where the advantages lie.

Where premiums are given for new or increased accounts, funds deposited in return for a gift must remain for a specified period, such as 14 months. A penalty may be enacted for early withdrawal.

If you are planning to leave the area where you have savings accounts, remember that you lose interest if you close a regular savings account before the end of a quarter (or other period stipulated by the institution). You may also lose interest on a day-of-deposit to day-of-withdrawal account by closing it before the end of the interest period. A bank or thrift often calls for a minimum deposit to be left in an account to the end of the period in order to have interest posted. Note, too, that if, for example, a thrift offers 5.50 percent interest with an annual yield of 5.73 percent, the higher rate only applies when the account is left open until the end of the year.

A depositor leaving town but not in immediate need of funds may prefer to have a final check closing an account mailed at the end of the year when interest has been posted.

Withdrawals from term accounts where penalties are imposed are also discussed in this chapter.

Passbook Savings Accounts

While the passbook savings account earning interest at the rate of 5 to 5.50 percent is a useful device for putting budget money aside until needed and for emergencies, inflation and taxes on interest continue to erode such accounts. The saver withdraws shrunken dollars which buy less than when deposited. The transfer of funds to time accounts which pay higher rates in return for commitment for set periods will help the saver. However, until interest rates on savings are geared to inflationary times, the saver may be running hard but either standing still or losing ground.

A major problem in allowing banks and thrift institutions to pay higher interest rates to savers is the bind in which such financial institutions would find themselves. Lending is their business and when debts such as long-term mortgages are still returning only 7 or 8 percent, they do not want to pay more to savers. The fact that savings account depositors are subsidizing borrowers has been recognized and new types of accounts are likely to appear which will allow savers more flexibility.

Because depositors will always want ready access to a portion of their savings, passbook accounts will remain a necessity. Though some financial institutions apply fancy names to accounts, passbook accounts are generally either regular or day-of-deposit to day-of-withdrawal.

Regular accounts do not allow depositors to withdraw funds without loss of interest until the end of a quarter (or six-month-period). They may, however, have a "grace days" feature. Deposits made up to so many days from the beginning of a month or quarter earn interest from the first of the month or quarter. The number of grace days varies with the financial institution. Many allow 10 days each month, with 3 days each quarter allowed for withdrawals without loss of interest.

Day-of-deposit to day-of-withdrawal accounts, a more recent development, permit withdrawals at any time without loss of interest for the period. Interest is only lost on the amount withdrawn from the day of withdrawal. Usually, grace days are not offered, but some large savings and loan associations may extend this bonus feature.

Time Deposits

You may be familiar with time deposit accounts under another name, such as term savings account, certificate of deposit account, savings certificate, or a special name invented by a particular savings institution. The principle of this type of savings account is that money is committed for a specified period for advantageous rates; withdrawal before maturity means a penalty, as described below.

Because in times of inflation funds kept in passbook accounts may actually be losing money, it is preferable to put savings into time deposit accounts, using the term most suitable to individual or family goals. The saver can draw on the interest quarterly or annually at a sacrifice of some interest. For example, you choose to place $5,000 in a 7.75 percent time account for seven years; the effective annual yield is 8.17 percent. The higher figure applies only when interest is left untouched. If you draw upon it, the account pays 7.75 percent per annum.

Maximum rates are set by government regulation, but not all financial institutions pay those rates. Minimum deposits required to open time accounts are, as of July 1, 1979, set by banks and thrifts, not by regulation. Long-term advantageous rates may be obtained for deposits of $100, $250, $300, $500—at various financial institutions. Some still require higher minimums, $2,500, for example. Look for the most advantageous offerings in your area.

The minimum for the money market certificate described below remains at $10,000.

As of July 1, 1979, depositors may pool funds to secure better interest rates. For example, two friends may use their checks for $5,000 each to secure a $10,000 money market time deposit. The bank is allowed to pay the same rate of return as for a single depositor's funds. A bank may not advertise for pooled funds, solicit them, or form groups of depositors who want to pool funds. However, it may accept such funds; it may also limit the number of savers in a group.

Rates that have obtained at thrifts on time deposit accounts for a considerable period are 7.75 percent (8.17 percent effective annual yield), on a 6 to 7 year commitment of funds; 7.50 percent (7.90 percent) for 4 to 6 years; 6.75 percent (7.08 percent) for 4-1/2 to 5 years; 6.50 percent (6.81 percent) for 14 months to 2-1/2 years. Some thrifts also offer 5.75% (6 percent) for 90 days to 1 year. These are the maximum currently allowed; a particular financial institution may offer less; at times, a bank or thrift may cease to offer the maximum, reinstituting it at a more favorable time.

In 1978, thrifts were permitted to offer a new time account, yielding 8 percent (8.45 percent effective yield) for funds committed for 8 years or longer. The same year saw the innovation of 6-month savings certificates tied to the weekly rate of 26-week Treasury bills on minimum deposits of $10,000. The thrift

institutions were permitted to offer ¼ percentage point more
which, in addition to compounding of interest, gave the saver a
better deal than at commercial banks. The banks were tied to the
Treasury rate although they might also offer compounding of
interest. Early in 1979, regulations changed and ceiling rates
instituted which made the offers less attractive for savers although
financial institutions preferred the limitations. Compounding was
no longer allowed and the ¼ percent differential between commercial banks and thrift institutions was eliminated. However, if
rates dropped below 9 percent, the thrifts were permitted to offer
as much as 9 percent while the commercial banks were tied to the
actual Treasury bill rate.

Savers must always be alert to changes in the types of accounts
offered. Because small savers demanded better opportunities for
their funds, a new type of time account became available as of July
1, 1979, with a 4-year or more maturity; minimum deposit as
required by the issuing bank or thrift. The ceiling rate is
established monthly for accounts opened that month, and is based
on the average for certain Treasury securities. Commercial banks
may pay 1¼ percent below this average rate, thrifts 1 percent. As
the new type account began in July, 1979, thrift institutions were
offering 8.28 percent effective annual yield on 7.85 percent,
commercial banks 8.01 percent on 7.60 percent annual interest.

Give instructions regarding interest. If you want interest to
remain in your account for compounding and crediting, say so on
opening the account. Banks have been known to automatically
transfer interest to customers' regular or day-of-deposit accounts
each quarter, thereby lowering the annual yield. If you wish the
interest to be sent to you each quarter, you can, of course, give
instructions to that effect.

Watch maturity dates. Banks and thrifts should notify customers when time deposits are becoming due, and offer options of
payment, renewal, or transfer to other rates or accounts. You
should receive the notice in good time so you can deal with it by
mail or in person. However, not all banks or thrifts fulfill this
obligation to the customer. A large New York City bank for savings
has failed in this way, while competitors have wisely sent out
notifications, thereby gaining customer confidence. All time

deposit savers should keep a record of when their accounts are coming due. If instructions to a bank are not given in time, the maturing funds may be transferred to a day-of-deposit account at lower interest, or automatically renewed. While the automatic renewal feature may be a useful option, the depositor may wish to place funds from maturing accounts to better advantage.

Income tax on interest earned on a time savings account is not deferred even though you may not draw on the interest until the account matures. You receive a report of interest from the savings institution at the beginning of each year and enter the sum on your Form 1040 in April.

Pre-Maturity Withdrawal Penalty

Government regulations impose a penalty on savers who withdraw principal from time accounts before maturity. All types of savings institutions are required to inform the customer of penalties for early withdrawal.

A penalty long imposed has been the loss of 90 days interest, plus the reduction of the rate of interest paid on the amount withdrawn to passbook rate. This penalty remains in force for time deposits issued up to the end of June, 1979. As of July 1, 1979, new and renewed time deposits are subject to changed penalties. Where the original maturity of the account in question is one year or less, the minimum penalty is loss of three months interest on the amount withdrawn, or interest since the date of deposit, whichever is less. On certificates of more than one year, the loss of interest is for a 6-month period. However, these are minimum penalties; a bank or savings institution is permitted to be more severe. Savers should always be sure they are informed of penalty rules in effect for a new account.

In case of death, a bank or savings institution is permitted to release funds to the depositor's estate or representatives without penalty. Time accounts opened as of July 1, 1979, come under a new regulation. In case of death, "no penalty" becomes mandatory.

Do Not Neglect Your Account

Do not be misled into thinking that a passbook is sufficient and perpetual proof of your ownership of funds on deposit. It is not. Every state, to some extent, practices escheat, that is seizure of property with no apparent owner. One of the most common forms of escheat is acquisition by the state of unclaimed bank deposits.

Depending upon the state in which the bank is located, an account that has been dormant for a number of years becomes vulnerable to the laws of escheat. (In New York, the time is now 5 years.) If a bank fails to reach a depositor through the mails at his last known address and through advertisements and public notices, it must turn the funds over to a state after its defined number of years (often 10) has elapsed. Once the money has been handed over to the state, securing its return is an involved procedure.

To safeguard your savings, you should keep a record of all your accounts, the numbers, banks, and locations. At least once a year (preferably more frequently), have the bank enter interest in each passbook you own. If you move, notify every bank in which you have an account of your new address.

Another little publicized fact is that savings accounts dormant for a number of years may cease earning interest. In addition, a savings institution may, under its rules, pay no interest on balances below a set minimum, which minimum can change without a depositor's knowledge.

Savings For the Holidays

Commercial banks, mutual savings banks, and savings and loan associations run Christmas and Chanukah clubs, generally based on a 50-week coupon book. The customer decides the amount to be deposited each week and the bank or savings institution will issue a check when the club matures, generally at the end of October. Some banks now offer clubs for 50 weeks that start at any time of the year.

Before opening a club account, find out if interest is paid and at what rate. Banks and thrift institutions may offer the same rates they pay on their day-of-deposit to day-of-withdrawal accounts - which generally means lower rates obtain at the commercial banks. Some banks and thrifts impose penalties for failure to complete a club; some deny interest. However, today's trend is in favor of more liberal policies than in the past. Not long ago clubs did not pay interest, and the weekly amount always had to be the same. Look for the club best designed to suit your own savings plan.

Interest on Checking Accounts

There are now ways in which interest can be earned on checking accounts, but not all bank customers do or should take advantage of the opportunity. Interest-bearing checking accounts come in a number of different varieties according to the banks or thrifts which issue them and it is not easy to decide which may be advantageous.

The first types of such accounts were Negotiable Orders of Withdrawal (NOW), which began in New England in 1972. At first confined by law to banks and thrift institutions in those states, NOW accounts came to New York State in October 1978, and are expected to spread further. Their arrival in New York coincided with the November 1 launching of Authorized Transfer Service (ATS) at banks across the country. In consequence, where NOW accounts were permitted, ATS were generally abandoned in favor of the NOW system. Both are described below:

Negotiable Order of Withdrawal (NOW) accounts. Initially, these interest-bearing savings accounts operated at no charge, but by 1978 expenses caused the imposition of minimum balances, generally similar to the ATS accounts, though some thrifts tend to have lower minimums and there is a new prevalent interest rate ceiling of 5 percent, annual rate 5.20 percent. Technically, negotiable orders of withdrawal are not checks but operate in the same way. The saver has no separate checking account. For this reason, NOW accounts are cheaper for financial institutions to offer than ATS.

A NOW account customer who wants a passbook loan or cashing of third party checks may find they are not permitted under this type of service.

Authorized Transfer Service (ATS). You may never see this term if you go to a bank offering the service. Banks tend to label their own offerings with special names which may confuse a customer, but the result is the same. The customer has both a checking and a savings account but funds are kept in the interest-bearing savings account until needed when they are automatically transferred into the checking account. Banks and thrift institutions usually impose minimum balances for savings, from $500 upwards; often $2,000 or $3,000; some have transfer fees, some check fees. Usually fees apply if the balance falls below the minimum. Interest is 5 percent, currently. Only by inquiry and looking at advertisements can a potential customer discover what a particular bank or thrift is offering. It is then up to him or her to figure out advantages.

In the spring, 1979, a federal appeals court ruled illegal the payment of interest on checking accounts by ATS and under other payment plans. Congress, said the court, had to decide the issue. The effect of the ruling was delayed until January 1, 1980 to give time for Congress to act, but resolution still may not be forthcoming by then. Meanwhile, the bank, thrift, or credit union customer can go on using the services offered. Possibly Congress will simply legalize the current situation.

Should you use an interest-bearing checking account? In general, anyone who has been keeping a high balance in a noninterest-bearing checking account may benefit by switching to an ATS or NOW account. But customers in the habit of maintaining a low balance and writing many checks may find that fees, penalties for dropping below the minimum, to say nothing of the taxes to be paid on the interest, add up to a costly program. If, at a financial institution in your area, a low minimum balance is required for a NOW or ATS account, and any fees and charges are reasonable, the convenience of such a plan may make it advantageous.

Nevertheless, many people like the old separate system for the good reason that they intend savings for future use and use checking accounts to pay bills. They prefer not to mix the two.

Special Checking Account Plans for Seniors

Many banks and thrifts offer advantageous checking account terms to senior customers, sometimes in association with the automatic deposit of Social Security checks. Some financial institutions call for the establishment of a minimum savings account. In states where NOW accounts are permitted, seniors may find banks or thrifts offering them no-charge checking/saving.

The definition of "senior citizen" may vary. In some areas, age 60 qualifies an individual to senior privileges; elsewhere it may be age 62 or age 65. Seniors, whether working or not, should inquire at banks and thrifts about no-fee or low-cost checking.

United States Savings Bonds

Savings bonds backed by the credit of the United States Government continue to play a role in the financial security programs of millions of American families; more than $50 billion worth of these securities are currently outstanding. In addition to patriotic reasons, people have been attracted to investing in savings bonds for one or more of these reasons:

1. United States E bonds can be redeemed at a stated value on demand after two months from the issue date; H bonds after six months. New rules apply to Series EE and HH bonds (described below), issued after January 2, 1980.
2. These bonds have been a "liquid" reserve, quickly and easily translated into dollars and cents when needed. Only EE bonds will have this feature in future. Penalties apply in the case of HH bonds.
3. Savings bonds are not subject to market fluctuations; they are never redeemed for less than the amount invested.
4. Interest on savings bonds is not subject to state or local income or personal property taxes.
5. The Federal income tax on Series E bonds and now EE bonds interest can be deferred; the annual increases in value need not be reported on the Federal tax return until the bond is cashed.
6. If savings bonds are lost, stolen, or destroyed, they can be replaced without cost.

7. Savings bonds are easy and convenient to buy. They are sold at neighborhood banks and savings institutions. Also, many corporations have established payroll savings plans; an employee can buy bonds regularly merely by authorizing his employer to make automatic deductions from his pay check.

On the other hand, there are certain disadvantages to savings bonds as a form of investment:

1. Although the Treasury has several times raised the interest rate for savings bonds, bond rates have generally lagged behind savings bank rates, and continue to do so. The Treasury has authority to pay up to 7%, but at the time this book went to press the current rate was 6.5%.

2. Savings bonds cannot be used as collateral and cannot be pledged. If the money is needed, the bonds must be cashed and an immediate tax incurred not only on the current but also on the accumulated interest on which tax has been deferred.

3. Compared to other investment, such as securities or real estate, savings bonds offer neither growth potential nor capital gain possibility. The lack of growth potential, coupled with inflation, is considered the greatest disadvantage of savings bonds as an investment.

Types of Savings Bonds

Series E and Series H bonds have long been sold by the Treasury. From January 2, 1980, Series EE and Series HH will be sold instead. However, sales of the old savings bonds continued until that date and present holders have options concerning redemption. All the bonds are described below.

Series E Bond. This most widely-held bond has been sold over the years at 75 percent of face value with a limit on a year's purchases of $7,500.

Series E bonds mature five years from their issue date. As of June 1, 1979, E bonds have 6.5 percent interest if held to maturity; they yield less if redeemed earlier because a low interest rate obtains during the first year.

Series E bonds can be cashed in at most banks prior to maturity if they are at least two months old. Generally, no notice is required. These bonds are not negotiable and cannot be used as collateral for loans. They must be in registered form. Registration may be in the name of a single owner, adult or minor, with or without beneficiary, or in co-ownership form.

Hitherto, holders of E bonds could obtain ten-year extensions on maturity. Now, E bonds bought from 1941 to April 1952 on which extensions have been granted, come to final maturity between 1981 and April 1992; no more interest will be paid and holders will have the option of redeeming and paying tax due or exchanging for new HH bonds, as described below, and continuing to postpone tax payment. Series E bonds issued after April 1952 are allowed another 10-year extension. It has been announced that E bonds purchased in 1979 can earn interest for up to 25 years.

Series H bond. The H bond was an income bond, sold in denominations of $500, $1,000, $5,000, and $10,000, maturing 10 years from its issue date. The Series H bond is priced at par or face value and is redeemable at par. While the interest on the E bond accrues to maturity, H bond interest is paid every 6 months by check. As of June 1, 1979, interest is 6.5 percent.

New rules state that interest ends on Series H bonds bought before July 1959 and which mature between February 1982 and May 1989. These old bonds must be cashed on maturity. However, H bonds bought after June, 1959, are allowed one more 10-year extension on maturity. Up to 30 years is allowed on H bonds purchased in 1979. Series H Bonds will not be exchangeable for the new HH bonds. December 31, 1979 is the final sale date for present Series E and Series H bonds but sales of E bonds under payroll programs end June 30, 1980.

Series EE bond. Replacing Series E bonds, the new EE's sell after January 2, 1980 in denominations of $50 through $10,000, with the annual accumulation set at $15,000. Because the price will be half the face amount, $25 will, for example, buy a $50 EE bond. But the waiting time until maturity becomes 11 years and 9 months, with a ten-year extension allowed. A buyer of EE bonds who wants to redeem soon after purchase must wait six months before action may be taken.

The interest rate for EE bonds is 6.5 percent, an average rate at maturity, building up from 4 percent in the first year and reaching a steady 6 percent after five years, as with the old E bonds.

Series HH bond. The replacement bonds for Series H selling after January 2, 1980 may be accumulated up to $20,000 a year face value. Interest is a steady 6 percent. Denominations are the same as for H bonds; also the 10-year maturity period, but HH bonds now carry a penalty factor, designed to discourage redemption before maturity. But there is no penalty on exchanges for E or EE bonds.

Naming beneficiaries. Buyers of the new EE and HH bonds may change or delete the name of a beneficiary without notifying such a person (or persons) or obtaining consent to do so.

Tax aspects of savings bonds. The exchange of maturing Series E bonds for a like amount in Series H bonds has been a popular device over the years. Payment of tax could be postponed on the E bonds while the new H bond holder paid tax on the semi-annual interest received. An older person could legally avoid E bond interest tax until death—when his or her estate would have to pay. The exchange of E bonds for H bonds during 1979, however, would not be advantageous because of the replacement of the H bonds. An exchange of E bonds for the new HH bonds after January 2, 1980 would be a wiser tax move.

New law will now prevent E bond holders from deferring tax on interest indefinitely. As noted above, E bonds bought before May, 1952 stop earning interest on maturity (between 1981 and 1992). Tax will have to be paid on the accumulated interest unless the bonds are exchanged for the new bonds. Such an exchange will continue the tax-deferral device.

However, you may decide not to defer payment of tax on interest on your E bonds but report the increase in value on your return each year. If you have accumulated E bonds for some years without paying tax and make the decision to pay annually, you may elect to do so and include all the accumulated interest on which tax has been postponed. But once you have made such an election, you would need approval of the Treasury before you could change that method of reporting.

Income tax can also be saved if you buy E bonds regularly in the name of your son or daughter for college education expenses. (Be sure you do not list yourself as co-owner of the bonds, but you may be the beneficiary.) The interest is taxable to the child - who probably will not owe enough for Federal tax to be payable; but you may file a tax return to report the accrued interest. When the bonds are sold at college time, the child pays no tax because the interest was reported annually.

Saving With Uncle Sam

Many people turn to "Treasuries" for two reasons: interest is not taxed at the state and local level; the investment is secure, being backed by the full faith and credit of the United States government.

But buyers should use judgment—buying at a time when interest rates are favorable; also, they may need substantial funds for some Treasuries, such as T-bills which are issued in minimum amounts of $10,000 and multiples of $5,000 above. On the other hand, some bonds and notes are available for $1,000 minimum. Maturities run for 13, 26, and 52 weeks on bills, two to 10 years on notes, more than 10 years for bonds. Interest is in discount form on the popular Treasury bills so that, when the average price is established from an auction, the buyers receive a quick return in the mail.

When investors in Treasuries need their principal before maturity, the bills, bonds, or notes must be sold on the secondary market. Here, there is risk of loss if the timing is unfavorable. On the other hand, the seller can reap profit. (Experienced buyers go into the market for this purpose.)

For the newcomer investor, Treasury bills have a great deal of appeal because principal is available again in 13, 26, or 52 weeks, and there is less risk of having to turn to the secondary market for a quick sale in case of emergency. At a time of rising interest rates, rolling over short-term issues can be advantageous because a new, higher rate can be obtained. However, investors turn to longer term Treasury issues when rates are falling to nail down the best interest yield available.

How to buy Treasury bills. T-bills may be bought through Federal Reserve Banks and branches, directly from the Treasury, or, at a charge, through a bank or broker. The procedures described below for direct purchase from the Federal Reserve Bank in New York may differ from procedures in your area. It is therefore a good idea to make inquiries at the nearest Federal Reserve bank or branch on the steps to be taken.

Noncompetitive tenders are usual since the price quoted on a competitive tender might be too low, leading to rejection. You can submit your tender personally or by mail any business day before the auction, which is usually on Mondays (Fridays in case of Monday holidays). While it is best to complete a form, obtainable from the Federal Reserve Bank, tenders may be made by letter so long as the following information is given:

1. The face amount of the bills you want;
2. the maturity you want (3, 6, or 12 months);
3. whether you are submitting a noncompetitive or competitive bid and, if competitive, the price;
4. whether you want to reinvest your funds at maturity;
5. the account identification, which includes your name and mailing address;
6. social security number(s) (two social security numbers are required for co-ownership);
7. your telephone number during business hours;
8. your signature.

Payment in full face value of the bill or bills must accompany the tender, usually by certified personal check or official bank check such as a savings bank teller's check. Treasury securities maturing on or before the issue date of the new bills may also be used.

Your account with the Treasury. You will hear by mail a few weeks after buying your T-bills that the Treasury has established your account. You will then be able to advise any changes regarding reinvestment, payment of principal at maturity, new address or ownership, etc.

Formerly, because T-bills come in bearer form, you had to keep them in a safe-deposit box or other secure place. If stolen, they could be sold. Now, you have the choice of placing your securities in a Treasury book-entry account, making arrangements for redemption or roll-over at maturity without risk of loss. About 80 percent of Treasury securities are held in book entry. There is no charge for the maintenance of this record.

The Treasury does not handle any sale of its securities before maturity. People who wish to sell must request that a transfer be made to a commercial bank which can handle the transaction. Buyers who anticipate sale through the secondary market may prefer to take delivery of their securities as before in order to make such transactions easier.

Buying Treasury notes and bonds. You may obtain information on buying from the nearest Federal Reserve Bank or branch; that branch would, on request, notify you when bonds are to be sold since there is no regular schedule. Notes are sold more frequently. Watch financial publications for news of these events.

While T-bills are discounted, so that buyers receive an immediate return shortly after purchase, interest on both notes and bonds is paid semi-annually.

Taxation of Treasuries. Although interest escapes tax at the state and local level, Federal income tax must be paid. Any loss or gain is considered ordinary, not capital, loss or gain even if on bills held more than 6 months.

Obligations of U.S. Agencies

In addition to Treasuries, the conservative investor can turn to the obligations of various federal agencies. Some of these obligations carry full faith and credit of the United States, some only an implied guarantee, some have no backing from the Federal Government. Although the 100 percent guarantee enjoyed by Treasuries is not available for all these agency obligations, risk is generally considered negligible. Potential investors are less acquainted with these issues than with Treasuries and they do not sell as readily on the secondary market. These factors add up to a higher return on the issues.

Some, but not all, agency obligations escape income tax on the state and local levels.

Purchases of agency obligations are made through commercial banks or brokers, at a similar charge to Treasury issue purchases. (Where the charge is the same for large, long-term transactions as for small, short-term purchases, the investor must consider the effect on his overall yield.) The U.S. agency securities generally have minimums of $5,000 or $10,000, but some may be available as low as $1,000. Or units of certificates (for example, Government National Mortgage Association (GNMA) pass-throughs) can be bought for $1,000. Inquire about the different types of obligations issued by Banks for Cooperatives, Federal Home Loan Bank, Federal Land Banks, as well as GNMA and FNMA (Federal National Mortgage Association), and other agencies.

CHAPTER 3

Using Credit Wisely

Today, it is the rare person who does not use credit in some form or another. Credit, the right to incur debt and defer payment for merchandise and services, is so readily available now that it can be either a blessing or a curse, depending on how you use it. Overextending yourself through easy credit terms means trouble if you lose sight of your obligation to pay. With so many desirable things available, you may be tempted to buy now and worry later. With inflation and taxes eating away at income, you may easily overestimate what money is really available for purchases on credit.

As long as you recognize that credit represents a debt you have to pay, and you are prepared through your financial planning to pay within the stated time, you can enjoy immediate possession of department store goods, plane tickets, gasoline, rental of a car, accommodation in a motel, and countless goods and services merely by showing a card and signing a bill.

Your Credit Rating and Credit Bureaus

To get credit, you must be a good risk. Thus, your credit standing is a major asset to protect. You build up your standing over the years and take it with you when you move. From coast to coast, credit bureaus pass along information and confirm or deny your ability to meet your obligations.

When you apply for credit, your rating is generally referred to a credit bureau, a company whose sole business is to check credit references.

If your credit application is turned down, do not consider your case closed. It is your right, and your obligation, to know why you have been denied credit. The company denying your credit must inform you of the credit bureau that supplied the data. You may see this information at no charge if you request it within 30 days after credit has been denied. Inaccurate data must be verified and a new report furnished to creditors. If you do not agree with the report after reinvestigation, you may include your own written statement explaining the information to which you object. Note that negative credit information - failure to pay a bill - should be removed from a record after 7 years; judgments and lawsuits against you may generally remain on file for only 10 years and, after October 10, 1979, bankruptcies must also be removed after 10 years.

Even if your credit rating remains unchallenged, you are permitted to review your file. A nominal fee may be charged. You may inquire about your rights under the law by writing to the Bureau of Consumer Protection, Federal Trade Commission, Washington D.C. 20560 or the Office of Saver and Consumer Affairs, Federal Reserve Board, Washington, D.C. 20551.

Applying for Credit

A department store, the bank, or finance company will require you to fill out a form and to satisfy an interviewer as to your character, your financial resources, and your capacity to pay. You will be asked for the name of employers, past and present, to state your salary and other income, and to give details about home mortgages or rent, bank accounts, and your charge or credit cards. If you, as an applicant, choose to offer the receipt of alimony, child support or maintenance payments as income, the creditor must consider such income; you are not required to reveal such sources if you choose not to.

See to it that your answers to questions will stand investigation. If you fail to give full or truthful information, you will damage your credit record, and that is a fatal step in financial mismanagement.

Credit may not be denied on the basis of sex or marital status nor on race, color, religion, national origin, or age; nor even on the basis of receipt of public assistance. Thus, women can obtain credit in their own name, regardless of their marital status. Single women will not lose their credit standing when they marry, nor will married women lose their rating when divorced or widowed. Creditors may not ask any questions regarding child bearing. This means that mortgagers must consider a wife's income, whether full or part-time, when considering the couple's credit before granting a mortgage.

Credit Cards Give Easy Access to Credit

Credit cards and their use have multiplied in recent years. Many businesses, from department stores to oil companies, issue their own cards for purchasing their goods and services. However, many businesses issuing their own cards will also accept bank cards. Travel and entertainment card organizations such as American Express, Diner's Club, and Carte Blanche, have added many incentives such as free travel accident insurance, cash, and check guaranteeing services to their use at better restaurants, theaters, high class stores and luxury hotels, but charge an annual fee in addition to the credit charges. Bank cards which do not charge an annual fee, such as Master Charge and VISA, often suffice since they are accepted by stores, hotels, motels, airlines, and many types of businesses and services in the United States and abroad.

Because of the ease of using a credit card, you should discipline yourself to keep account of how much you are charging, where, and when. In this way, you will know how much will be needed to cover the inevitable billing. When bills are running too high, you should limit credit card buying to a specific level each month to keep payments under control.

Also ask yourself: Is it really necessary for you to delay your payments? Consider that the cost of delaying payment may be as much as 18 percent a year which can mount up alarmingly fast.

What you save by paying promptly could add up to a useful sum in an education or vacation fund.

If you do not know just how and when you are going to pay for the merchandise, gasoline, services, entertainment, or travel charged, you should get yourself on a strictly cash basis until you can bring better order into your financial affairs.

As a rule of thumb, to see if you are carrying a safe amount of consumer debt exclusive of your home mortgage, compare your net income (take-home pay) to the following percentages: 10 percent or less to pay debts is safe; 15 percent—reconsider before increasing debt and work to reduce your present level to the safe 10 percent; 20 percent or more is a dangerous level. If 20 percent or more of your after tax income is going to pay off consumer debt, perhaps you should consider seeking professional advice. You may contact the Consumer Credit Counseling Service in your area or, if there is none, you can write to the National Foundation for Consumer Credit, 1819 H Street, N.W. Washington, D.C. 20006, for the names of a counseling service near you.

Guarding Against Misuse of Credit Card by Others

Dishonest clerks or merchants can misuse your credit card without your being aware of their fraud. If the card is taken from view during the billing, the clerk has the opportunity to make additional copies of your plate on sales slips. A cash purchase is later billed on one of the slips, and your signature forged. The clerk steals the cash; you get the item on your statement. Always compare your duplicate sales slips with the charges on the statement to make sure they are correct. If there are discrepancies, be sure to follow through on your rights, as explained below.

To protect yourself against the misuse of your credit card by others, at the time of transaction, you should see that the sales slip is accurate. If errors require a new sales slip, see to it that the old one is destroyed.

If you lose your credit card, you are liable only up to $50 for unauthorized use of your card. However, as the $50 is on a per card basis, your liability may be sizeable if you had several credit cards lost or stolen and subsequently misused. You can limit your liability to zero if you report each card loss prior to any unauthorized use. Keep a list of the telephone numbers to be called in case of loss, along with your credit card numbers. Follow up the call with a letter.

If, after reporting a loss, you find the missing cards were only misplaced, also notify the companies immediately. The numbers of your cards will be on an alarm list and using them could place you in an embarrassing situation.

Credit card insurance coverage may be bought separately or, in some cases, added to personal policies such as homeowners or casualty policies. You may at the same time acquire other benefits, such as insurance against loss on altered checks, but you may also have to prove that you handled your cards with due care and immediately reported loss. Inquire about company rates and requirements; they differ widely.

Handling Disputed Charge Account Bills

The bill from use of your credit card must be mailed at least 14 days before you must settle it. In the past, a customer might incur interest charges simply because his bill arrived too late for his payment to be recorded.

If you question a charge or the amount of a bill, you should call the telephone number supplied on the bill. Some problems can be handled promptly by phone. If your question persists, you should pay the undisputed portion of the bill and pursue a speedy resolution to your problem through the mail. The creditor must answer your letter within 30 days and your complaint must be resolved within 90 days. An address must be given on the bill for inquiries and complaints. Moreover, open-end creditors must identify each transaction on the monthly statement.

No collection letters may be sent while a bill is in dispute, and the creditor must inform the credit reporting agency of the state of affairs so that no unfavorable credit rating is issued on an unresolved matter. When the dispute is concluded, the credit bureau is informed. If a creditor fails to comply with the requirements of the law, the penalty is forfeit of the amount of the bill, up to $50, even if it was not in error.

A credit card holder can withhold payment in respect to defective merchandise over $50 in value and purchased within 100 miles of his home, and need not be held liable for the entire amount owed. Formerly, a bank or credit card company involved as "third parties" in credit transactions were protected against a consumer's complaint when redress could not be obtained from the merchant.

Your Charge Account at Department Stores

Stores use different types of accounts, according to their class of business. With the *Open* or *Regular Account*, you buy from stores in person, by mail, or by telephone without down payment or service charge. But the statement which you receive is marked "payable in full within 10 days of receipt of statement." In practice, this works out as a 30-day period.

The above type of account is being superseded by a variety of accounts, all of which carry some form of interest charge on the past-due balance, depending on the type of contract you entered into. Penalties are usually incurred for not paying by a specified time after receipt of the monthly statement.

Titles of accounts vary from store to store, and it is not always possible to say which title fits which method. Some retailers combine different forms of payment into their installment contract. For example, one national company's *Revolving Charge Account* contract permits the customer several choices: First, he may pay within 30 days, no penalty. Or, second, if he fails to so pay, he automatically becomes liable for a 1-1/2 percent per month charge on his outstanding balance. He then remits whatever installment payment is due according to a set schedule. That is, if he owes $50, he may have to pay $10 a month, but if he runs his account to $200, he pays $20. Finally, he can also pay in advance.

Another form often described as the *Revolving Credit Account* works this way: The customer agrees with the store credit department on an amount to be paid monthly. The store then sets a limit on purchases so that the amount outstanding will not exceed the original set level. Debts above the agreed amount must be paid immediately.

The *Retail Installment Credit* agreement of a famous coast-to-coast store operates as a Regular Charge when the bill is paid before the next statement date. Otherwise, the customer has to pay a service charge of 1-1/2 percent per month and at least 1/6 of his current balance. Ten dollars is the minimum monthly payment.

A well-known discount department store has been operating *Regular and Budget Accounts* for some years. At one time, such stores worked only on a cash basis. Now, the store offers a three-way option account: You pay the entire balance; you pay the current minimum amount due, according to schedule; or you pay any amount in excess of that minimum. The finance charges vary slightly over the states served by the store, according to local law.

The 1-1/2 per month charge has been common in the retail business on bills to $500 with a reduction to 1 percent per month on larger amounts. Some states impose restrictions which reduce the annual percentage that may be charged. You should ascertain the current rate allowed in your state.

Many companies and department stores have *Easy Payment Plans,* under which the customer pays a presettled amount each month to cover interest and principal, the debt being settled in a limited time, say, 12 or 24 months. Such installment contracts are further discussed below. Generally, they are for big items, such as automobiles or appliances, usually described as "durable goods."

Payment of Credit Accounts

A problem with the payment of various types of credit accounts has been the imposition of service charges on amounts the customer had already paid. Sometimes the trouble arises because the payment has not reached the company's accounting department before the next billing period. But some stores deliberately use this type of billing, especially on revolving charge accounts. Under this "previous balance" system, the customer's partial payments are not deducted when interest is computed. If the store used the "adjusted balance" system, taking payments and credits into consideration before computing interest, the customer would pay less interest.

Some states have rules against the use of the previous balance system, but allow companies to use the "average daily balance" in computing bills. Under this plan, the customer does get credit for his payments, but he is charged interest in proportion to the time his balance was not reduced by the payment.

If you have a complaint about a store's billing practices and can get no redress, make your complaint known. Some local newspapers and radio stations handle such consumer grievances. You can write to the Federal Trade Commission, or your state attorney general.

Bank Credit Plans

Bank credit plans vary in detail, but not in substance. One plan establishes the borrower's right to credit of up to $5,000. The borrower does not actually receive any money. He makes use of the available credit whenever he pays his bills with the special checks issued to him. He pays a monthly interest charge on the amount of credit he actually uses, and for the checks. As he repays the amount borrowed plus interest, he establishes his right to use the credit again.

Another system does not require special checks. A borrower of good standing may write a check for more than he currently has in his account. But, because he has arranged for the bank to set up a credit reserve of between $400 and $5,000, his check is met. Repayment each month is subject to a minimum amount, usually $10, and more checks can be written, thereby adding to the debt. The annual percentage rate of interest is typically 12 percent. More than one type of repayment plan is available. A bank customer can have this checking account for years and never use the credit feature, but it is available if he needs it.

In such bank credit plans, the borrower may be required to meet standards of credit even more stringent than those required by a bank in making conventional type loans. The loan proceeds are not turned over to the borrower under either of these plans. Instead, the loan comes into existence when the arranged-for credit is used - by writing of a check. With a regular bank loan, the borrower describes his purpose, which must be approved. Under these plans, the borrower uses the credit as he pleases.

Bank Debit Cards

As the names imply, with credit cards, you are using someone else's money to pay your obligations, but with a debit card, also called a cash card, you are using your own funds. With the advent of electronic machines to facilitate sidewalk transactions, your bank may offer you a debit card so you could have access to your funds after banking hours. While you do not incur interest charges, because you are merely using your own money, you should be aware of the possible problems and costs to you for possessing a debit card.

In case of loss, you can limit your liability for unauthorized use of your card to $50 if you notify your bank within two business days of loss. If you report the loss between the second and 60th day, you may be liable for up to $500 of unauthorized losses. If you fail to notify the bank after 60 days, you are without recourse should your entire account be wiped out.

In addition to costs for unauthorized use of your card after you lose it, a new card may be intercepted and used without your being aware of it. Always arrange to pick up a new card in person. Store your personal identification number in a safe place and do not keep a copy of it in your wallet or purse. If you cannot commit it to memory, you are asking for trouble. Finally, do not discount the fact that some thieves and muggers may station themselves near a cash machine and wait until after you have withdrawn your cash before accosting you. You then must shoulder the loss without recourse to the bank. To emphasize again, these potential problems are mentioned to alert you to what can occur in order to assist you in deciding on the use of debit cards.

Installment Buying

One of the most important points about your savings program is that it enables you to pay cash for the goods you want instead of paying someone else additional money for a loan or time plan. This is where your planned goals serve you. You decide that next year you will need a new car, or a refrigerator-freezer. You could go out and obtain the desired goods now at the cost of installment payments, or you could save the money at interest in a day-of-deposit to day-of-withdrawal savings account until you had the purchase price. Here, you would have to weigh your actual need of the item - essential now or deferrable to the future, the pace at which you can save, the interest rate at the savings bank weighed against installment charges - and the possibility of a rise in price. You should be aware of the economic factors currently obtaining so that if, say, the price of certain appliances is rising, a good installment contract is worth more than saving against a rising tide of costs. An alternative is to get a bank loan for major purchases.

Reviewing the Installment Contract

If you are considering an installment sale purchase, consider such points as:

Your ability to make a substantial down payment. A large initial payment will reduce the spread of payments and the charges you would be paying. If you do not have the means to make that large down payment, think twice about whether you should be undertaking the installment payments.

What will your other commitments be during the period you would be paying on time? Have you left yourself a cash margin for emergency? Certainly it is not possible to safeguard against all eventualities, but it is the too heavy load assumed for too long a period that drives many families into debt from which they cannot easily escape.

The repayment period. Interest charges mount up during the spread-out-paying period. Choose to pay as quickly as you can. The shorter the period of repayment the lower the overall cost. And, too, consider the length of time the item purchased will be useful to you; do not commit yourself to a term of repayment that exceeds the usefulness of the item. For example, do not plan to pay off a car in four years that you do not expect to keep beyond three years.

Under the law, before you sign any installment contract, you must be told:

1. The cash price of your purchase and the deferred payment price.
2. The amount of the downpayment, or that none is required.
3. The number of payments to be made, the amount of each, and the due dates or period of payments.
4. The amount of the finance charge expressed as an annual percentage rate.
5. The amount of penalty, if any, for prepayment of your debt and how the unearned part of the finance charge is calculated; what penalty would be imposed if you are late with your payments, or if you entirely default. Take note that even if the buyer is entitled to repossess the goods, it may not relieve you of your obligation to pay.

In addition, you must be furnished with a copy of the contract and a notice of cancellation. Before signing anything, however, make sure all the blank spaces have been filled in. Keep the copy of the contract in a safe place.

Whether a contract is offered to you by a ready-money lender, by a store where you are to pay on the installment plan, or by a door-to-door salesman, you should know that the contract is likely to be sold to a third party such as a bank or sales finance company. Where the customer pays on time there is no trouble, but when he or she fails, the buyer of the contract has the legal rights set out in the contract; he may repossess the property, take over any security, have the debtor's wages garnisheed, or a wage assignment made. The contract may hold you liable for costs and the creditor attorney's fees if you are taken to court over the debt. And, finally, the credit bureau will be notified and this will affect your ability to get credit in the future.

Federal and state laws, as well as various consumer groups, are gradually coming to the aid of bewildered consumers who have failed to fulfill contracts that they have signed. In some cases, the contract did not set out the debtor's rights as required by law; often the debtor did not fully understand what he signed;

frequently the penalty is excessive, as where the goods are repossessed and the debtor is still liable to pay for them. Nevertheless, the weight of the law is still likely to be with the creditor. The best protection any consumer can have is to go slow on signing a contract, to check its points, to consider the legal commitments.

Familiarize yourself with the laws in your state concerning consumer recourse in the event of faulty merchandise. If you are buying on the installment system and the merchandise proves defective, you may only have a limited time in which to lodge a complaint. Once that time is passed, you have no redress; you still owe installments on a faulty or useless item.

When You May Cancel an Installment Contract

You have time to reconsider a contract you have just signed. You may cancel the transaction before midnight on the third business day after the date of the transaction. The seller must furnish you with a notice in large clear type telling you of this right to cancel, give you the form on which to write the cancellation, and details of his business name and address for its safe delivery.

If you have already taken delivery of the goods, you must arrange with the seller for their return in good condition; he is responsible for any expenses of shipment. If you fail to return the goods as arranged, then the terms of the contract will stand and not be cancelled. On the other hand, if the seller receives your notice of cancellation and arranges for the pick-up of the goods, and does not do so within 20 days, you are under no further obligation to return them.

When you cancel, the seller must return to you any payments you made at the time you signed the contract. He has 10 days in which to do so.

If You Need a Loan

If you find that you need a loan to meet an emergency, to purchase a house, a business, a car, to finance education, or to replace a pile of small bills by one large one, shop around. Terms and interest rates vary. Similarly when money for loans is tight, you may not be able to borrow at the first bank or institution you turn to, but do not give up. If your credit rating is good, you should be able to locate a source of funds.

Even if you are not presently in need of a loan, acquaint yourself with the availability and terms of loans from various lending institutions. The uninformed, worried, and hurried borrower is the most likely person to buy himself more financial trouble in the shape of an unnecessarily expensive loan.

If you, through no fault of your own, do not have an established credit rating, raising a loan may be difficult. Here, your resource may be a person who has the required financial standing. If you can find such a friend or relative to cosign a note at a bank or finance company, you get your loan. Your *comaker*, who personally believes in your integrity and ability to repay, has taken equal responsibility for settling with the lender if you should fail to do so.

It might be added here that if you are asked to cosign a loan, do so only if the borrower is a relative or friend you know well and in whom you have complete confidence. And, too, be confident of your ability to pay in the eventuality you are called upon to do so. Even a cosigner's credit rating may be in jeopardy if the borrower defaults.

Small Loan Companies Should Be Used as Last Alternative

Most states require small loan companies to be licensed. In this way, you can be satisfied that they are reputable and operating within the law.

Typically, loan companies keep usual business, as opposed to banking, hours. And, too, processing your loan application may be faster and less involved. But in return for speed and lack of intensive questioning, you will pay their high interest rates. If funds are borrowed for a short time, say, 6 months, make sure you determine the annual interest rate. This is explained later in this chapter.

The small loan company can assist the person without a credit background to consolidate debts and thereby to improve his future standing. Some will provide competent budgeting and counseling services which are of real benefit to people who cannot see their way through a difficult financial situation.

In general, go to the small loan company only if you cannot get a loan from a lower-rate source. If you do so, check on the company first. This can be done through the local Better Business Bureau.

Borrowing on Your Life Insurance Policy

Your life insurance policy may make a ready loan available to you at exceptionally low interest rates. Read up on your policy; cash value and loan rates will be stated. Write your company, giving your policy number, and state how much you want. (You can borrow most of the cash value.) Usually, a check will be sent within a few days, no questions asked, and you can repay on a system convenient to you. But be aware that your loan reduces your family's protection in the event of your death. The very lack of pressure to repay an insurance loan is not in its favor on a long-term basis. By constantly postponing full discharge of the loan, you heighten the risk of being underinsured. You also lack that cushion of financial assurance your insurance policies offer should you have to meet an even greater emergency in the future.

Your Savings Bank May Be a Loan Source

When the need for a loan arises, the person who saves regularly at a bank or savings and loan association has an advantage. If he has a day-of-deposit to day-of-withdrawal savings account, he can do without a loan and, instead, draw on his account for the needed funds; the only cost is the interst he loses while the money is gone. The good money manager will arrange to repay his account on a regular basis as if he had borrowed from an outside source. However, if you have a regular savings account where withdrawals can only be made at the end of a quarter without loss of all interest for the period and you need money right away, or you require the discipline of loan payments to maintain your savings account intact, consider a passbook loan. The savings bank will advance you the sum you need at a comparatively reasonable rate (for example, 2 percent above the savings account rate) and, at the same time, you do not lose the interest accumulated in your savings. All the time you are repaying the bank for your loan, your regular savings bank interest will be paid by the bank. The cost of the loan is essentially the difference between the interest rate charged and the rate you continue to earn on your account.

You may be required to repay your loan in monthly installments over one to three years at some banks while, at other banks, the manner of repayment largely is left to the discretion of the borrower. Self-discipline is important here to avoid mounting interest charges.

Borrowing From a Commerical Bank

Bank credit cards have made a difference to bank loans. Where installment loans were once touted, today many banks prefer a customer to use his bank credit card for small loans, say, up to $2,000. This type of loan may be called a cash advance. You pay the interest rates permitted in your state, usually from 12 percent to 18 percent a year. And you may pay interest on interest. This occurs where you fail to pay your monthly balance so that you incur interest on it. Next month that interest is added to the balance you owe, and interest is figured on the total amount, not only on your debt. The legality of card fee compounding is as yet unresolved. Ascertain the current policy at your bank.

The diligent borrower who wants the more advantageous rates of an installment loan for his home furnishings and appliances or for personal needs may find a small bank will offer better terms than a large one, and that both are open to negotiation on those terms. Typically, the loan for a TV set, say, will be over 24 months, while an unsecured personal loan must be settled in a year, and often costs more. The cost of automobile loans generally runs lower and may be spread over 24, 36, 48 or 60 months. If, at this time, you were applying for a secured car loan of $5,000 at one commercial bank in a New York City suburb, you would pay 10.33 percent over a 24-month period. The amount of your note is

$5,555.52 and you pay $231.48 a month. If you need 36 months in which to pay for the $5,000, the finance charges are $881.68 in addition to the $5,000 principal and you pay $163.38 a month, annual rate, 10.88 percent. Over a 48-month period, the finance charge on $5,000 rises to $1,249.60, your monthly payment drops to $130.20 and you pay an annual rate of 11.40 percent.

Not only do rates vary widely in different parts of the country, they vary as much in the same general area. Some banks will not offer loans in a specific category, e.g. autos, consumer goods, or personal; some will offer loans at the same percentage rate in all three categories. Do not be impressed or intimidated by banks' advertised rates; go in, inquire, and negotiate.

As discussed above, the cheapest loans will usually be those secured by collateral, or passbook loans from your thrift institution.

Mortgages and home improvement loans are traditionally the loan areas of savings and loan associations and savings banks; educational loans are also available at many thrift institutions.

If you are a veteran, you may be eligible for a G.I. Business Loan. While your first approach would be to go to the local office of the Veterans Administration, you would probably find the bank makes your loan through its participation in the G.I. Bill lending program. Terms are better than those offered to other borrowers.

Once again, it must be said that because of the variation in terms offered, you should shop several banks for the specific loan you want.

Borrowing From a Credit Union

Members of credit unions are able to secure loans at varying rates of interest. State and federal law sets the limit of interest rate but some credit unions charge below that limit. A credit union's rates may vary for the class of loan, with a maximum set by law. Generally, the credit union member can get better loan rates than are available from other lending institutions.

The solvency of a credit union may be affected when a large number of members fail on their loan repayments. A federal insurance plan and other safeguards are now in effect, and credit unions are better able to make the loans for the "provident and productive purposes" for which the organizations were established. These purposes include loans for medical bills and funeral expenses, weddings and home purchases, household repairs, starting a business, and taking vacations.

If You Put Up Stocks and Bonds as Collateral

If you own stocks and bonds and you need a loan, you have ready security for a bank loan. The bank holds your stocks, and you sign a "time note." This note may become due before you are ready to repay, but if your securities still have high market value, you will probably be able to have your note renewed. You only pay interest on whatever periodic basis you arrange.

You should be alert, however, to several factors in this type of loan. You do not get the current market value of your securities as a loan. The bank will offer less as a protection against possible decline in value. You will not be asked to put up additional security unless the stock drops to below the actual amount of the loan.

If you cannot pay the loan but the value of your stock has increased, the bank will sell all or part of your stock. It collects the debt, you collect some profit.

Your pledged stocks and bonds still bring in your usual dividends, and these may help to offset the cost of your loan.

Of course, when you repay a secured loan, your stocks or bonds are returned to you.

Credit Costs and True Rate of Interest

If you decide to buy on credit or to borrow money, you will want to know how much it is costing you to use the lender's money - both in terms of dollars and rate of interest. Then you can compare the varying prices of credit and be able to buy and borrow at the lowest cost. Or you might find that you cannot afford to use credit - the price may be beyond your means.

The law requires the lender to disclose the annual percentage rate and other pertinent information. However, some companies still fail to comply with the law and generally take advantage of customer confusion and ignorance. To aid you in making wise decisions, we include here a discussion on figuring interest rates. By substituting current figures for our examples, you will better be able to check on the costs of a loan or installment purchase.

Types of Loans and Ways of Stating Interest

When you "buy now, pay later," "charge it," buy "on time" "use a payment plan" and whenever you take out a loan - you are using someone else's money - and paying for the use of it. How much it costs depends on the terms of the credit agreement.

Simple interest. A loan at simple interest at 6 percent a year means that you pay 6 cents a year for each dollar you borrow. If you borrow $100 at 6 percent for a full year and do not have to make monthly installments, you would have the full use of the money until the end of the year. At the end of the year, you would repay $106. You would then be paying a true annual interest of 6 percent. If you repaid the loan in 6 months, the interest would be half, or $3. Six percent simple interest comes to 1/2 percent a month.

Discount loan. On a discounted loan, the bank discounts or deducts the interest in advance. On a $100 discounted loan, instead of $100, you are handed only $94. On a loan for a year quoted as 6 percent per $100 you have to repay $100. Each monthly installment comes to $8.33. Your true annual interest is 11.8 percent. If you repaid a $100 discounted loan over an 18-month period, the true annual interest would jump to 12.5 percent.

The discount method actually works out to a higher rate of interest than the add-on loan because the same $6 of interest is a larger share of $94 than it is of $100. Roughly, true annual interest on such a loan to be paid back in monthly installments over a year is about double the amount stated.

Under the law, the true annual interest must be disclosed to you. But if you wish to determine the figure for yourself, you can do so by applying the following formula:

$$\text{True Annual Interest} = \frac{\dfrac{2 \times \text{number of installments in year}}{} \times \text{\$ cost of loan}}{\underset{\text{actually received}}{\text{Amount of loan}} \quad \underset{\text{installments} + 1}{\text{Total number of}}}$$

Say you take out a loan of \$1,000, quoted at 6 percent per \$100 discounted, to be repaid monthly over two years. This means you receive only \$880. \$120 is the cost of the loan. You figure the true annual interest by applying the above formula as follows:

$$\text{True Annual Interest} = \frac{2 \times 12 \times \$120}{\$880 \times (24 + 1)}$$

This works out to 13.1 percent true annual interest.

Or, say you plan to purchase a washing machine costing \$300. The dealer offers you \$25 for your old one as a trade-in and quotes you a price of \$36 to cover carrying charges to finance the purchase over an 18-month period. You can check on the true annual rate of interest you would be paying by applying the formula:

$$\text{True Annual Interest} = \frac{2 \times 12 \times \$36}{\$275 \times (18 + 1)}$$

The finance charges on the washing machine would come to 16.5 percent in true annual interest.

As a result of law changes requiring disclosure of annual interest rates discount loans are increasingly less popular and are being displaced by add-on loans.

Add-on loan. On an add-on loan, the interest charge is added to your loan or purchase. On a 6 percent per \$100 loan for a year you have to repay \$106. If you make monthly repayments, you do not have the full use of the money for the entire year. Month by month, you have less, but you are still paying on \$100 at 6 percent a year. If you repay the \$100 plus 6 percent interest in 12 monthly installments of \$8.83 each for a total of \$106, your true annual interest is 11.1 percent, almost double what you thought you were paying. If your repayments are scheduled over 18 months, you would be repaying $109 (6 percent per year for 1-1/2 years). Your monthly payments would be lower, $6.05 per month; your true rate of interest would be higher, 11.4 percent.

Unpaid balance - monthly interest. Credit unions and small loan companies, as well as retail merchants and banks on certain types of charge plans, quote charges as a percentage of the balance unpaid each month. The true annual interest rate must be disclosed. You may check up for yourself by multiplying the monthly interest by 12.

Monthly rate	True annual rate is
3/4 of 1%	9%
5/6 of 1%	10%
1%	12%
1-1/4%	15%
1-1/2%	18%
2%	24%
2-1/4%	27%
2-1/2%	30%
2-3/4%	33%
3%	36%
3-1/4%	39%
3-1/2%	42%

As you repay the amount borrowed, the size of the loan decreases. For example, say your unpaid balance is $120 and is repayable in 12 monthly installments at 1 percent per month. Figure your interest charge on the unpaid balance at the end of the month as follows:

Divide $120 by 12 to find the amount of principal you must repay each month:

$$\$120 \div 12 = \$10$$

Determine the 1 percent a month interest charge payable on $120, your unpaid balance at the end of the first month:

$$\$120 \times 1 \text{ percent} = \$1.20$$

Your first payment is $11.20; $10 principal and $1.20 interest.
Subtract your monthly principal payment from the balance:

$$\$120 - \$10 = \$110$$

The second month you would repay $10 of principal and 1 percent interest on your remaining balance of $110 or $1.10. The second month you pay $11.10.

Figure your payments of principal and interest this way each month. Remember, your principal payment remains the same; the interest charge decreases as your unpaid balance gets lower. Your final payment of the loan will be $10.10.

This $120, 1 percent a month loan, actually costs 12 percent per year in interest; in dollars it costs $7.80.

CHAPTER 4

Buying Your Own Home
Or Condominium

New or used single family dwellings are particularly in demand despite sky-high prices. People see housing shortages as continuing and expect no end to the rise in construction costs. A single family house is still regarded as one of the best investments, one that will bring useful tax breaks while building up equity, and is likely to increase in value.

Condominiums provide a needed alternative, coming in different styles, some best suited to families, others to singles, childless couples, and retirees. Whether townhouses, garden apartments, or high-rises, condominiums offer the same opportunity for appreciation as single family homes and similar tax breaks may be obtained.

In addition to discussing general and financial considerations of home or condominium buying, this chapter will cover financing your purchase with old and new types of mortgages, protecting your investment with insurance, and special features of condominium purchases.

Should You Buy a House?

Say that in your search for a home, you have to decide between an attractive apartment and a small house. Both offer adequate room space, but the house offers a garage, front lawn, and backyard as well. You compare the apartment rent, plus rent for garaging your car, with taxes, heating costs, mortgage payments, insurance, and general upkeep of the house. You should include an estimate for repairs and redecoration. Take into account the cash payment you will have to make on buying and expenses of closing title moving into the house. The house appears more costly, but you get more for your money. And, under a long-range analysis, the house will probably turn out to be less expensive because of the economic advantages home ownership offers. These are (1) tax deductions, (2) build-up of equity, and (3) possible increase in value.

Tax deductions. When you pay interest to a mortgagee, and taxes on real property, you become entitled to a tax deduction for the amounts paid in arriving at your income tax liability.

If you have cash for a down payment on a small home, figure out what the net cost of carrying it would be over a five-year period, as compared with the rental you would have to pay for comparable quarters. You will probably find, as many others have found when they get a 20- or 25-year mortgage, that, after considering the income tax reduction for mortgage interest and taxes paid, the home actually costs less than the apartment. Moreover, in most instances, you will then own an asset of considerable value. On the other hand, you have nothing at the end of a rental term.

(If you are a veteran, local law may provide you with a partial exemption from property taxes. This will provide a reduction in the amount of monthly payments you will have to make to the mortgagee.)

Build-up of equity. Each payment you make to the mortgage includes amortization. This amount reduces your indebtedness under the mortgage, and in effect amounts to a form of savings. Many a homeowner has financed his child's college education by refinancing the home in which he has, over the years, built up an equity.

Increase in value. If real estate values continue to rise as they have in the past, and there is no indication of a reverse trend, your investment could be further enhanced.

Is Renting Better for You?

Quite aside from other financial considerations in the decision of whether to rent or to buy is the one concerning the use of the money "tied up" in the purchase of a home. Most real estate dealers will be prepared to show you how much you require in the way of monthly payments to finance your house. However, these monthly schedules of payments on mortgage, amortization, and other costs of home ownership do not include the amount you would otherwise be earning on the money you invest as a down payment for your home. For example, if you have to take $20,000 out of your savings to make a down payment, you will no longer be earning interest of $1,100 or more on that sum. Few analyses of the cost of home ownership take this into consideration.

There are times when it pays, very definitely, to think in terms of rental rather than home ownership. Take the case of the retired couple who are selling their large and greatly appreciated family home now that the children are gone and they no longer require so much room. The tax break offered homeowners over the age of 55 means that most of the gain on the sale will escape tax. Should they then seek a smaller, more convenient house to buy? Perhaps a house in another, less expensive, or more retirement-oriented community? True, they now have the cash with which to purchase this smaller home. But consider: Suppose they have sold their house for $100,000 - unlikely as it seemed when they bought it for $20,000 twenty years ago. If they put that $100,000 in a bank or in government bonds, or money market funds now offering a return of 8 percent or more, they will have an annual return of over $8,000 a year. This sum will very likely be sufficient to rent a comfortable apartment or house in most communities. In some, it will be possible to rent a suitable place for considerably less. Thus, the sum received on the sale of the house will finance the payment of comfortable living quarters whose upkeep is the responsibility of a landlord, rather than themselves. And the original nest-egg from the sale of the house remains untouched. They are in the enviable position of "living on income."

Inspect the Community and Its Environs

When you are considering a home in an unfamiliar location, investigate accessibility to shopping, schools, places of worship, and recreation areas. Even if you have no children, the quality of the schools will affect the price of the home should you decide to sell it in the future. Note if public transportation proves a viable alternative to driving, and if travel time to work would suit you.

When you are considering a specific house, try to talk to neighbors, not only to find out if they seem congenial but to learn about the district and, if possible, the house or condo you are considering. Noise may be a problem, particularly if highways, railroads, or airports are in the vicinity. Local authorities may have to be consulted to find out if plans call for a new thruway or nearby industrial development which would hurt property values. Open space nearby may look inviting now, but a view-obscuring apartment building or busy shopping center may be in the offing. Zoning laws are of the utmost importance. Look for any signs of declining values, and try to ascertain why, in the case of used property, the sellers are really leaving.

Check List on Buying Family Home

You usually will find two or three houses in the right price range, each of which may meet most of your requirements. However, none may meet all of them. You must make a comparison of the good and bad features of each and resolve your decision by a compromise. Here is a check list of some of the points you should weigh:

Size and expansion possibilities. If the number of rooms is adequate now but might not be after a few years, is there room for expansion? Will zoning laws permit you to expand the house?

Topography of the lot. Is there sufficient level ground for the play area you require? Will abutting property make necessary a retaining wall? Is drainage adequate?

Public utilities. Will you have to maintain a well, or does the public authority supply water? Is garbage and trash removal a public service? Are the public roads near the house kept clear of snow and ice by a public service? What are the zoning laws in the immediate and neighboring vicinity? A home near an area zoned for commercial or industrial use will not be as desirable on a resale, and will depreciate more quickly in value.

Is the house near a traffic center, a main highway, or a transportation center? Traffic noises may make a home less desirable on a resale. But it must be weighed against the advantages of easy travel to work. Is the cost high for public transportation to work, shopping areas, places of entertainment and recreation, etc.?

Will you need a car to get yourself and your family to daily pursuits?

Is the house within walking distance of schools, place of worship, playgrounds and shopping areas?

Are there sidewalks for children who walk to school?

Do zoning laws protect the neighborhood from deteriorating?

Are the schools crowded? If they are, you can be sure your taxes will be increased to provide for new schools.

Will your children be bused to schools at a distance from your home? Check for yourself the location of the school your children will be eligible to attend. You may choose a house because of the educational standards of the nearby schools - only to find out a child at your address has to attend another school. Check also at the school on the availability of transportation. You may be just outside the one-mile or other distance limit. Your neighbor's child may be entitled to transportation, while yours may have to walk or be driven to school.

Are there sewers, or other public improvements in the area for which your house is likely to be assessed?

Have you gone into and around the house on rainy as well as dry days to look for water seepage, cracks in masonry around window sills and in the basement?

Will your car fit into the driveway or garage?

Is the electricity amperage adequate for the electric dryer, air conditioner, and other equipment you may wish to install?

Is the water pressure adequate?

Is the heating and hot water system a costly type? Is it in good condition?

What about other houses in the neighborhood? Are they

maintained with pride or ownership or are they run down? You will not enjoy your home or obtain a good resale price if it is the only well-kept house in a neighborhood of rundown houses.

Is the neighborhood stabilized or improving?

Is industry creeping toward the neighborhood?

Do the grounds require immediate planting, a lawn or landscaping, a retaining wall?

Is the price comparable to sales prices of similar homes in the area?

Is the type of house one that is readily salable?

Old vs. New

When you buy and move into a new house you find everything bright, fresh, clean, and modern. You may even have had the opportunity to choose some of its features, such as wallpaper, flooring, fixtures, etc., but only up to the amount the builder has allowed for these items. This is often so when you buy a home from a builder who shows you a model house and then finishes your house accordingly. Anything you want that costs more than the amount the builder has allowed will be put in at your expense.

Builders of new houses usually provide a bare lawn and no landscaping. They do not put in screens or storm windows or doors. You will have to take these items of expense into consideration over and above the down payment for the house. You will also have to weather the frustrations resulting from "bugs" in construction. When a house is new, and until it is "broken in," doors and windows may stick, outside steps may crack, heating and hot water systems may need constant adjustments, and the settling of the house may mean repainting or papering of walls and tile repairs in bathrooms. However, you will be able to finance the purchase of a new house more easily than an older house. You can get a 25-year mortgage more easily on a new house than an older one, and on a smaller down payment.

On the other hand, an older house has other advantages. It usually has a warmth, charm, and at least appearance of, if not actual, sturdiness not found in new homes offered at comparable prices. The older home will probably save you the expense of lawn, landscaping, screen and storm windows and doors. If the house is in a well-established neighborhood, the schools are not as likely to become overcrowded or inadequate as quickly as in the new development areas. Property taxes will probably not increase as quickly as in new communities. There may be an existing mortgage you can take over, and so save some financing costs. But an older house may need modernization, particularly in the kitchen. It might need walls knocked down to make way for a family room. You may have to repaint or redecorate even before you can move in. You may require rewiring to accommodate all your electric appliances. If this will make the cost of the old house more than a comparable new one, and you do not have the ready cash for modernization, it would not be wise for you to buy an older house.

In your search for a family home, you may find a house that meets all your requirements - except that it has no family room, and you also wanted an additional bedroom and bathroom. The price is right, low enough to allow you to add the three rooms. The land appears ample enough to accommodate the expanded house. Nevertheless, before you bind yourself to any purchase, make sure that the enlargement will not cause the house to encroach beyond the building line and will meet legal limits. Also, that the necessary permits for construction of the proposed addition will be granted by the local authorities. Ask the present owner to let you see his survey, showing the limits of the property he is selling. Consult the local zoning and building authorities. Get their advice as to whether you would be allowed to proceed with your project.

When you get title and are ready to proceed with the expansion of the house, you will need an architect, plans, a contractor, etc., just as if you were building the custom-built house discussed below.

One other consideration you should not overlook in choosing between a new and an old house: make certain the older house is in a neighborhood that is not deteriorating or becoming commercial in character. If it is, your chances of getting your investment back will not be as good as from a new house that is comparable in cost.

You Need a Lawyer

You should retain a lawyer as soon as your offer for the house of your choice is accepted. The purchase of a house generally represents the most expensive buy of your lifetime. It is economically unsound to "do it yourself" to save a lawyer's fee.

Many brokers ask buyers for a nominal cash payment as a "binder." Such binders are often construed as contracts without giving the protection a contract provides. It is better practice to sign nothing and make no payment. The seller's lawyer can get a contract up in a very short time. Tell the seller to have his lawyer get in touch with yours, and the contract can be signed within a few days. At that time you will make your down payment.

Your lawyer will see that all the terms and conditions of the sale are included in the written agreement. If you cannot complete your purchase unless you are to secure a satisfactory loan or mortgage, your lawyer will try to get such condition stated in your contract. If the seller offers such items as carpeting, curtains, appliances, garden equipment, etc. with the house, your lawyer will see that you get title to this personal property at the closing. A seller rarely gives anything not specifically provided for in the contract.

Some home buyers are under the illusion that the attorney representing the mortgagee will look out for their interests as well, and that a lawyer is an unnecessary expense. This is not so. The lawyer for the mortgagee is there to protect the lending institution, not you. If there is an encroachment or easement turned up on the title examination, such fact will affect your interest as owner but will not deter the mortgagee's lawyer from going ahead to give you the mortgage. The mortgagee's interest for the amount it advances will be adequately secured despite this encroachment. But this might affect the marketability of your title. If there is an open assessment against the property, the attorney for the mortgagee will not concern himself about who pays it, or if it is paid. But your lawyer will try to get the seller to pay at least a part.

If the seller has failed to complete certain work called for by the contract as of the closing date, the attorney for the mortgagee may not be concerned. But your lawyer will, for your protection. He will try either to get a part of the purchase price put "in escrow" pending the seller's performance or make some other arrangement for your protection. He might get an agreement that the seller can have the balance that is in escrow provided he completes the work on or before a certain date. On his default, the money would go to you for you to have the work done. If the seller has made representations as to construction, your lawyer will try to get them in writing, for your protection in your investment.

Your attorney can also find out whether the house you are buying is protected by FHA or VA rules obligating the builder to correct structural defects, or to make allowances for the costs of repairs.

An attorney is also essential to other real estate transactions as in the purchase of a condominium or cooperative apartment. Too, legal advice is needed in the purchase of a mobile home and its lot.

The Role of a Real Estate Broker

You do not incur any liability for broker's commissions when you consult a broker about buying a house. His sales commissions are payable by the owner who makes him his agent to sell his house. Consulting a local broker, who generally knows most of the houses that are on the market in his area, will save you a lot of wear and tear and expedite your search for a home. An active real estate broker generally knows the actual sales prices of homes comparable to the one you seek. A reputable broker will tell you these prices to guide you in your offer. He knows what lending institutions will finance the purchase of the house you choose, what the lending institutions look for in issuing credit on mortgages; how much an institution is likely to lend, and where you can get an FHA or VA insured mortgage, if you qualify. Brokers are generally more expert than a layman in the art of negotiating between a buyer and seller and know how to keep open negotiations after a buyer's offer of less than asking price is rejected by the seller.

On the other hand, don't rely implicitly in a broker's sales talk or enthusiasm for the house he wants to sell. There are some things you should check. Have an independent expert examine the property.

Get an Expert's Opinion

After you find the house you prefer above others, and the price is in the right range, get a building expert to examine it for you. (Look under Building Inspection Service in the yellow pages of the telephone directory.) The building expert will check construction, insulation, the roof, the water pipes, the volume of electric current for appliances, the heating system, and tell you whether there is any evidence of termite infestation - a hidden danger in every house. He will give you an idea of annual heating costs and what repair and maintenance costs you should anticipate. He might recommend additional insulation for savings in heating costs, or other work on the house that will insure years of maintenance charges. If any costs are to be incurred along these lines, you should take them into account in financing your purchase.

Inspectors are usually licensed professional engineers or registered architects. The fee charged varies widely, and may depend on the location of the property, its value, and its size. You should ascertain what is provided by the service. Will you get a check list as well as a written report? How many items would be checked? Any photographs? Some services provide a shorter written report than others but their check list is longer.

You may know an architect or engineer who will make the needed inspection, or be recommended to a qualified man. The local real estate board should be of help if you need it.

The bank or savings institution where you apply for a mortgage may send an appraiser before they back the property with a loan. If you get a mortgage covering 70 percent, that will be some assurance of the house's value. However, you will probably wish to have your own independent inspection. The areas in which problems are most likely to occur are the basement (wet), roof (leaky), hot water system (defective), and the gutters and drains which overflow, clog, or back up.

Initial Purchase Costs

In figuring how much cash to put toward a down payment, count on such initial expenses as these and reserve cash appropriately:

Home inspection. In buying a house, an inspection by a qualified individual or home inspection company is essential. You need a report on the condition of the roof, water system, sewage, general construction, and what major repairs may be necessary immediately or in the near future. Inspection would reveal evidence of termites or other defects which might preclude your buying that property, or serve as a basis for renegotiating the purchase price.

Survey. A lending institution is likely to insist on a survey which would reveal any encroachments against the boundary lines of the land sold - as might happen if a neighbor had put up a fence along property lines.

Title company insurance. Generally required by a lender, title company insurance certifies the title of the seller for the mortgagee. A buyer may also want similar insurance. The cost of title and mortgage insurance depends primarily on the amount of insurance protection and locale of the home.

Expenses of obtaining a mortgage. Among the expenses additional to the cost of a survey and title insurance are those for an appraisal fee paid to the mortgagee; expenses of its attorney for drawing the mortgage and other legal papers, recording fees, usually nominal, paid to the county, and any mortgage tax levied by the state.

Lawyer's fees. Before engaging an attorney, ask for his fee for representing you at the closing of title. If you think the fee is high, check with another attorney. There is nothing improper in shopping for the lowest fee. However, when buying a condo, engage a lawyer who is thoroughly knowledgeable in this highly specialized and relatively new field of law.

Advance payments on adjustments. On the closing of title, certain adjustments are made on taxes and insurance premiums. When an existing mortgage is assumed, interest must be adjusted. You must generally be prepared to pay in advance up to six months' real estate taxes and, to protect the mortgagee, insurance premiums up to three years.

Ask about all these items in advance so that you know where you stand financially before you commit yourself to something beyond your available funds.

How Much Should You Put Down?

In deciding how much cash to put down, consider several factors. The larger the down payment, the smaller your mortgage loan will be, and the less its monthly cost to you. In the very least, lenders require a minimum down payment, say 20 or 30 percent; some demand 30 to 40 percent. But VA - FHA loans may have substantially smaller down payment requirements of only 5 or 10 percent. Consider, too, that your loan will be paid back with inflation dollars. Thus, if your monthly payment is $400, and 10 years from now inflation has gone up 100 percent, your monthly payment will seem like only $200 to you, assuming that your income keeps up with inflation. This may influence you to put down as little as possible and carry as big a mortgage as is comfortable. Conversely, if you are on a fixed income, the inflation factor may dictate putting down as much as possible and keeping your monthly payments to a minimum.

Financing Your Home Purchase With a Mortgage

The purchase price of your house or condo, over and above the cash payment, is generally financed by a mortgage. The lender is the mortgagee; you are the mortgagor. In consideration for the money advanced to you to enable you to pay the balance of the seller's price, you pledge the house and land as security for repayment of your loan with interest. If you fail to pay your mortgage debt, the mortgagee may foreclose, that is, sell your house in order to pay off the mortgage debt.

There are several sources for mortgage funds. Mortgage money can be obtained from commercial or savings banks, savings and loan associations, life insurance companies, and other lenders, including individuals. The seller of the house you are interested in might take a mortgage on the house. This may be a possibility if he is not himself in need of immediate funds to buy another residence and you cannot get funds elsewhere. In such a case, the mortgage debt is known as a purchase money mortgage. The purchase money mortgage may be for the entire cost of the home in excess of a down payment or in addition to a mortgage secured through a bank or other institution.

A mortgage debt which the seller incurred when he bought the house may have a lower interest rate than currently available rates. You may wish to take over the seller's mortgage, that is, assume it. Where interest rates have changed, his lender may not let you take over the mortgage. The lender may, however, rewrite the loan perhaps at a rate more favorable than would otherwise be obtainable. You might check this possibility.

The amount of money you can obtain depends on such factors as the availability of money in the market, your credit, the age and condition of the house and its current market value, the number of years over which the loan is to be repaid, and the rate of interest. The area of the country in which you will live will have a bearing on the mortgage rate and upon the amount of the down payment required. Rates may also vary in favor of new housing as compared with previously occupied houses.

You may also have to pay points to get a mortgage. A point is equal to one percent of the loan and a number of points may be charged to, say, make up the difference between a FHA/VA insured loan and a conventional loan, or to otherwise get around borrowing at more than a state's maximum interest charges. However, regulations may forbid the buyer to pay points on FHA/VA loans; the way around any such rule is to have the seller pay the points difference in a lump sum; the price of the house to the buyer is raised to correspond.

Charges paid by a borrower are sometimes called points, and refer to a "loan processing fee," or some other term describing a charge for use of money. When points on a principal residence can be described as interest, they are generally deductible for income tax purposes in the year paid.

Time, Interest and Other Mortgage Terms

The time period and other terms of a mortgage depends on the age of the house and general economic conditions, and the policy of the financial institution. As you increase the time period over which your mortgage has to run, you reduce the monthly payment but increase total interest you will have to pay. For the near future, lower monthly payments may better suit your budget.

Although rates of interest vary in different localities and on the availability of money in the general market, you will generally find that most major lenders in a given area offer home mortgages at similar rates. Nevertheless, shop around. A difference of a fraction of a percent can mean an overall saving of several hundred or more dollars.

In addition to interest and amortization payments, the mortgagee may require you to pay a stated amount each month toward real property taxes into an "escrow account" from which taxes will be paid by the mortgagee. This monthly payment is subject to change in amount if taxes are increased. In any event, you must count on this, too, as a carrying charge of owning your home.

Keep in mind that the interest you pay on a mortgage loan is deductible for income tax purposes. The actual cost of a higher interest rate may be less than appears at first when you take into account this tax deduction over the mortgage term. It is only the *interest* portion of each installment that gets this treatment; principal is not deductible.

Prepayment. When negotiating for a mortgage, it is a good idea to get the privilege of prepaying it, preferably without a penalty. Some lending institutions may not allow you to prepay a mortgage. Some will allow prepayment on payment of a percentage penalty of the unpaid balance due. If you have surplus cash over your family needs and want to cut monthly living costs, it might be to your advantage to prepay the mortgage even on payment of the penalty.

If the interest rate on your mortgage is below the current rate, the mortgagee might waive the penalty and gladly accept your prepayment without it.

Finally, the terms of the mortgage will require you to maintain adequate fire insurance (at least an amount protecting the lender's interest), keep the house in good repair, and pay taxes promptly (the bank may take over this responsibility through an escrow arrangement).

Monthly Payment on Standard Mortgage
Per Thousand of Mortgage

	15 years	20 years	25 years	30 years
8½	9.85	8.68	8.05	7.69
9	10.14	9.00	8.39	8.05
9½	10.44	9.32	8.74	8.41
10	10.75	9.66	9.09	8.78
10¼	10.90	9.82	9.27	8.97
10½	11.06	9.99	9.45	9.15
10¾	11.21	10.16	9.63	9.34
11	11.37	10.33	9.81	9.53
11¼	11.53	10.50	9.99	9.72
11½	11.69	10.67	10.17	9.91
11¾	11.85	10.84	10.35	10.10
12	12.01	11.02	10.54	10.29

Example. You get a $70,000 mortgage for 25 years at 10-1/2%. Your monthly payments for principal and interest are $661.50 (70 x 9.45).

Federal Government Support of Mortgage Funds

Federal government policies may at times facilitate your request for a mortgage fund, and may offer better rates and terms, if available.

Federal Housing Administration mortgage. The FHA, a division of the Department of Housing and Urban Development (HUD), does not loan mortgage money directly. An FHA mortgage is obtained from a private lending institution, but this government agency insures the lender against loss in case of the home owner's failure to repay it. Some lenders may be willing to accept smaller down payments and a lower interest rate, and to lend their money over longer periods because of this guarantee. (However, when mortgage money is tight, lending institutions are less ready to handle loans insured by the FHA.) FHA charges a low insurance premium on the unpaid balance, included in the monthly payments the mortgage calls for. There is a dollar limitation on the value of the homes for which it will provide mortgage insurance.

When you buy a home and plan for an FHA-insured mortgage, the FHA will make a complete review of your ability to meet the mortgage obligations. This credit review is made after the bank or other lending institution willing to make the loan submits your application to the FHA. In addition to appraising the property, the FHA will consider your estimated continuing, dependable income, estimated prospective monthly housing expenses, and estimated living costs, debts, and other financial obligations.

Although government agencies are trying to process applications for home loans more expeditiously, these applications necessarily involve a great deal of paperwork. The biggest drawback to an FHA mortgage is that it takes longer to get than a conventional mortgage.

An FHA mortgage provides the home owner with a certain feeling of security not usually associated with bank or other corporate mortgages. FHA policy is to see that every effort is made to avoid foreclosure on insured mortgages where the owner is suffering a hardship because of unfortunate circumstances beyond his control. Lenders are encouraged to wait as long as a year from default before beginning foreclosure, to suspend payments or reduce the amounts temporarily, or to modify the terms for the payment of the unpaid balance within the owner's ability to meet them. If the lender is unwilling to enter into an appropriate "forbearance" arrangement with the home owner, the FHA can ask it to assign the mortgage to it, so that it can work out relief provisions suitable to the home owner's circumstances.

FHA regulations also include special relief provisions for military personnel.

Veterans Administration mortgage. If you are a veteran, you should check with the local VA branch regarding eligibility and opportunity for a VA-guaranteed mortgage. Generally, such a mortgage will run for a longer term, may have lower interest rates, and require a smaller down payment, even, in some circumstances, none. As with FHA loans, those insured by the VA are only granted for property meeting set standards.

Alternative Mortgage Terms

In a conventional (standard) mortgage, your interest rate and monthly payment remain constant. But in the earlier years of the loan, a greater part of each payment represents interest. Toward the end of the mortgage loan, the reverse is true, with the bulk of each payment representing principal. The standard mortgage is the most common type currently available. While it may be more burdensome to the lender in the first few years than some of the newer types of mortgages discussed below, it offers predictability and the lowest cost over the life of the mortgage.

You may also be offered one of the following types of newer mortgages as an alternative to the standard one:

Variable rate mortgage (VRM). Under the terms of a VRM, the lender may increase or decrease the interest within certain limits when shifts occur in money markets. A borrower's payments may change once or twice a year. In lieu of higher payments, the borrower may be able to elect to extend the mortgage terms. Generally, VRMs may cost the borrower more, so they have been opposed by consumer groups. However, they have not yet been fully tested in all parts of the country. Spreading from California where they were first offered by state chartered savings and loan associations, they are now allowed in a number of states; permission for federally chartered savings and loan associations to offer VRMs is anticipated at this writing.

When VRMs were first introduced, they were offered at slightly lower interest rates, but now rates are competitive with standard mortgages. It is argued in favor of VRMs that the protection offered to the lender through higher rates may encourage more financial institutions to lend more money. In turn, the amount of down payment required from a borrower should be lower.

Graduated payment mortgage. Monthly payments are initially smaller than under the standard mortgage on the same amount of principal, but payments increase each year over the first five- or ten-year period and continue at the increased monthly amount for the balance of the mortgage term. The smaller initial payments may allow families who expect future rises in income to get into home ownership now instead of later.

Because the debt increases instead of decreasing, this is known as "negative amortization." If the house is sold within the first few years, there may be less left over after paying up the mortgage than may have been expected. When compared with the standard mortgage, over the term of the loan, the graduated payment mortgage will cost more.

An open-end mortgage is one that provides that, during its term, the owner can ask for an additional advance to increase the unpaid balance for an extended period under the terms of the original agreement. This provision can be of great value in the later years of a mortgage, when the additional money might be needed to finance a child's education, to make major improvements, or for other purposes. The original face amount of the mortgage is generally the ceiling for the total of new and old loans. The mortgagor usually grants the additional loan if the value of the property, the owner's credit, and other circumstances warrant it. Even if an increased rate of interest was a condition for the extension, it would be less costly for the homeowner than refinancing through a new mortgage.

Balloon mortgage. In this type of mortgage, you pay off the loan for a set number of years, say nine years, as if the loan were a standard 20-year mortgage; in the tenth year, the balance is paid off by refinancing. Before entering into such a mortgage make sure you have an irrevocable assurance of refinancing on reasonable terms. Otherwise, you may be faced with the obligation to make a balloon payment with no funds to do it.

Reverse annuity mortgage. This is not a mortgage used to finance a home purchase, but, rather, a means of turning a fixed asset (a home upon which the mortgage has been paid) into liquid funds. The bank gives the home owner the value (or a percentage of the value) of the home and the funds buy an annuity which can be used to provide retirement income. Interest on the mortgage is paid back out of the annuity, but the principal is not repaid until the house is sold or the owners die.

Approval to offer such loans by federally chartered savings and loan associations was granted in January 1979. Some state-chartered thrift institutions have had permission to offer reverse mortgages for some time. As with other new type mortgages, RAMs may be permitted but not always readily available. It takes time for financial institutions to adjust to mortgage innovations.

Inflation Is a Major Homeowner's Insurance Risk

Today, the major insurance problem is not whether you carry insurance-most property owners do-but whether you are adequately insured. Sometimes under-insurance is caused by short-sighted efforts to cut corners but more often today under-insurance is caused by failure to take account of inflationary increases in the cost of replacing property. Construction costs have almost doubled in the last decade. A house that cost $30,000 to construct in 1969 may now cost over $60,000 to replace.

What can you do? First, realistically appraise the value of your property periodically and see that your insurance coverage reflects these values. Second, consider adding to your policy an "inflation protection" clause which increases coverage and premiums automatically on your house and contents by a set percentage based on the construction cost index in your area.

Home owner policies are standardized. There are six standard home owner's policies generally described by the abbreviations: HO-1, HO-2, HO-3, HO-4, HO-5, HO-6. Four policies are for personal residence, HO-1, HO-2, HO-3, HO-5; one for condominium owners, HO-6; one for tenants, HO-4. All of the policies cover common perils such as fire, vandalism, glass breakage and theft. They also give comprehensive personal liability coverages and provide for limited medical payments. HO-1 is the bare basic policy for home owners, while HO-5 is the most comprehensive policy. Ask your agent for a brochure which describes the protection features of each policy. Compare, ask his advice, and then decide whether the wider-coverage of a more expensive policy is worth the added cost in terms of risk and your pocketbook.

When you have decided which form to buy, check the premium rates. Call up several different insurance companies. Premiums vary because insurance costs are determined by the past experience of each company in the area; the construction type of your house and its closeness to a fire department.

If you decide to buy more extensive and expensive coverage, you may reduce insurance cost by raising the amount of the "deductible." You may save as much as 10 percent on your premium if you increase the deductible from $100 to $250. A $500 deductible might produce a 20 percent saving.

How much insurance should you carry. The land and foundation of your house are not insurable and in figuring insurable value, an average 20 percent of the value of the house is generally allocated to land; five percent to the foundation. This leaves 75 percent of value to the house. To allow for full coverage of losses in case of partial damage to your house, you have to insure up to 80 percent of the value of the house. For example, if the value of your house (not counting land and foundation) is $75,000, you should insure the house for at least $60,000 (80% of $75,000). If you insured for less than $60,000 and you suffer say, damage of $5,000, the company would pay only part of the damage based on a ratio of the insurance carried and what should have been insured under the 80 percent rule. However, even where you meet the 80 percent test, recovery for a total loss is limited to the face amount. To protect for a total loss of your property, the face amount would have to cover 100 percent of the value of the house.

"Floaters." Where the coverage of your standard home owner policy is inadequate for certain property losses, such as jewelry, you can add a "floater" for additional protection for such items.

Flood insurance. Flood insurance may be available under a government-subsidized National Flood Insurance Program (NFIP). NFIP coverage is offered by the Housing and Urban Development Department (HUD) for areas that have undertaken flood control protection. The amount of available insurance depends on the status rating given to your area. When a community first qualifies under the NFIP program, it is in emergency status, and during that time, you can buy up to $35,000 of flood insurance on a single-family dwelling; coverage for the contents of your house up to $10,000. After premium rates are set in your area, emergency status ends, and you may then buy up to $185,000 of coverage on the house and $60,000 on the contents. All types of buildings, including commercial, may be insured under the program.

Is a Condominium For You?

Ownership of a condominium unit gives the buyer certain advantages that go with single family house ownership and, for a maintenance fee, association dues, or monthly assessment, some of the pluses that go with apartment dwelling. All maintenance chores are handled; snow-shoveling, lawn mowing, gardening, street repair, etc. A staff repairman may be on call for jobs to be done in a unit although the owner must generally pay for the work. Strong security is often a selling feature of a condo; some have high walls, guards at the gate, patrols, or closed-circuit TV. An owner usually pays the costs of utilities. In high-rise condos, these may be included with the maintenance fee.

The tax advantages to condo ownership are the same as those for single family houses. Mortgage interest and property taxes are deductible. Property taxes are based on an owner's percentage of common elements and are assessed on each unit and paid direct.

Of course, if an owner sells his condo unit in a poor real estate market he may suffer a nondeductible loss, just as the owner of a single house might do.

Who runs a condominium? The job of running the condo is left to the association of owners. The association handles the maintenance fees, collects from slow-payers, enforces the rules, and through its treasurer (or an accounting firm), pays insurance premiums, taxes, bills and salaries. In larger condos, the owners often employ a manager or a real estate company for this purpose. Some developers, instead of relinquishing all hold, keep a finger in the pie through hidden ownership in a real estate firm which obtains a long-term management contract. Such arrangements may result in high fees and poor service.

If you are buying a condo on resale, the seller will tell you who runs the development. But check with other condo owners to determine the performance of the managers. If you are buying a new unit, try to discover if the developer plans to be involved with the management of the condo. In either case, as an owner, be prepared to attend association meetings and possibly to run for election to the association board.

Are maintenance charges reasonable? Sometimes, in a new condo a developer will hold maintenance charges down until his units are sold. After he has left, the owners find mounting costs make higher monthly assessments necessary. Local officials may be able to clue you in as to reasonable charges. If you are buying on resale, try to ascertain if major expensive repairs are coming up with subsequent increases in the monthly assessment.

Investigate the developer and the law. In considering a new condo, investigate the developer. What is his reputation? Inquire locally of the Better Business Bureau; contact the state's real estate commission and the office of the attorney general; if necessary, get in touch with the U.S. Department of Consumer Affairs in Washington, D.C. An area office of the Department of Housing and Urban Development (HUD) may be in a position to give you background information. Also find out if your down payment is protected. A deposit should be placed in escrow. If you allow your funds to be co-mingled with those of the developer, and he fails to sell all his units or leaves his development part-built, your down payment may be lost.

Acquaint yourself with your rights under state or federal law. Some states have lagged in protecting condo buyers against abuses. In New York, state law is tight; in Florida, where condo growth is particularly heavy, new law has been slow to catch up with buyer need. Across the country, legislatures are having to deal with various aspects of condominium abuse. The protection that may be offered by local law on conversions of apartments to condominium ownership is discussed below.

In new condos, you must check out what the salesman promised. All the condo plans should be on file with the County Clerk. Developers and their salesmen may play down local real estate taxes, promise recreational areas and fail to supply them, underestimate closing costs. You may be told you have free use of garage space, the pool, the tennis courts, or other recreational facilities, but in fact you find the developer has retained rights that compel you to pay "rent" for what you thought you owned. Finally, determine whether the developer controls the utilities. Where this is so, rates may zoom for inadequate service, and the owners lack redress.

In a resale, ask the seller to show you the master deed and the rules by which the property is governed. This information will help you determine if the condo fits your life style with regard to children, pets, and guests.

Have you talked to the neighbors? If you are buying a new condo, whether or not you have seen a model unit, you should try to meet residents of finished units and ask if they are satisfied buyers. Sometimes model apartments are not representative of actual apartments, being made to appear larger and, of course, faultless. When you yourself are not among the first residents of a project still under construction, you have the opportunity to gain information you need. If you are buying a resale, talking with prospective neighbors will help you learn what the seller may not tell you: problems in the development and prospects for the future.

Should you buy a condominium on conversion? The rate of conversion of rental apartments into condominiums is high; building owners have found it to be a profitable way of disposing of their interest and some tenants believe that tenant-owned buildings will be run better, while giving the investment and tax advantages of home ownership. But not all tenants may wish to or can afford to support conversion. As a result, controls have been imposed by some state or local authorities. Such areas often require that 35 percent of building tenants must agree before an landlord may convert. Protection of senior citizen tenants from eviction may also be proscribed by law.

What if, like it or not, your building is going to convert, and you must decide whether you will buy your apartment or move? Or you are condo-seeking and are considering buying a unit in a just-converted apartment house. Does this old building represent a wise choice? In answering this question, you will certainly want to know how the building compares with newer condo property. Depending on local law, the owner may have to provide a report on those elements of the building which will be owned in common, as well as on specific units, and supply warranties. Sometimes old buildings receive surface beautification which may be misleading; the pipes and wiring may be unsound.

If you are a present tenant, you may know the assets and flaws of the building, and be in a better position to judge your apartment as an investment than a newcomer. If you find units are sticking on the market and you have alternatives, you may not want to commit yourself to the purchase; you have to consider your position on resale. Comparison with new condos will be a guide. For example, if a converted building lacks soundproofing to be obtained elsewhere, both present tenants and prospective buyers may question the investment value of the unit.

CHAPTER 5

Your Investment Program

Investors traditionally turn to the stock market to increase their capital and income at rates exceeding the return offered by savings institutions or low-risk obligations. Others play the market as they would a roulette table. They gamble for winnings and appear willing to risk losses. The name of the stock market game for both the investor and speculator is risk. You must decide whether your personal and financial situation permits the taking of risk. The young career man or woman and older people without dependents may feel less need for caution than those with financial responsibility for others or the retired who cannot afford loss.

In your particular case, only you can judge whether to run the risks of the market. To help you in considering the market as a source of investment return, we present basic information. Investment opportunities in options and commodity futures are not discussed, since high risk ventures should be left to sophisticated investors and specialists. Investments in mutual funds are discussed later in this chapter.

What Are Securities?

If you are new to stock investment, read the following section.

You need to know the difference between common stock and preferred stock and the difference between stocks and bonds.

Stock. When you buy stock of a corporation, you are investing money in the company; in a sense, you become part owner of it. In return for your investment, the corporation generally pays you dividends out of its earnings and profits. If the corporation is successful, the value of your shares of stock may increase. Any increase in value of your shares is not taxable until you sell them. On the other hand, if the corporation does poorly, you may receive few or no dividends and your shares of stock may decline in value. Other factors including general economic conditions and public confidence also affect your stock; your shares may decline in value even though the company itself is making money and growing.

There are two classes of stock, common and preferred. (For investment purposes, stock may also be graded according to the company's business reputation and dividend-paying record.) Holders of common stock participate in the concern's profits or losses. Preferred stock is the senior stock of a corporation and its dividend is usually set at a fixed amount. The claims of preferred stockholders come after company bondholders' and take precedence over those of common stockholders. Thus, if the company goes bankrupt or liquidates, bondholders' claims on the company's assets come before those of preferred stockholders. The interest due on the company's bonds takes precedence over the dividends on its preferred stock. Claims of holders of common stock come last.

However, in terms of safety, the preferred stock of one company may be a "safer" investment as regards assets and earnings than the bonds of another company. Usually high-grade preferred stock provides a steadier dividend income than common stocks. Common stocks, on the other hand, offer greater opportunity for appreciation.

Convertible securities. Convertible securities are issued in preferred stock or bond form. They are called convertibles because the preferred stock or bonds can be converted into common stock of the issuing company at the election of the investor. As a rule, the convertible privilege is included in the provision written into the bonds or preferred stock itself. There are some issues, however, which are convertible as a result of a detachable warrant issued with the security, usually a bond.

Conversion privileges and terms vary with the particular security. The convertible preferred of one company might be convertible into one share of its common stock, while that of another company might be convertible into three shares of its common stock. Also, the conversion privilege might continue indefinitely or be limited to a period of time ending on a specified date.

Investors often choose convertible securities for capital gains and a hedge against market decline. As a convertible security is either a bond or preferred stock, it has a senior position in the company's capitalization before common stockholders are paid off. If the stock market drops, these securities are sometimes less vulnerable to the decline. Thus, danger of a large capital loss with tax limitations is lessened. Since the convertible can be converted into the common stock, its value moves up as the value of the common rises. In fact, once parity point is reached, its capital gain potential is enhanced over that of the common stock. A convertible preferred that can be exchanged for three shares of the common stock will jump three points on every one-point rise in the common once the parity point is reached.

A convertible generally will command a premium over and above its intrinsic worth. You must pay something for the conversion privilege.

Bonds. When you buy a bond, you are lending money to the issuer of the bonds. You do not become an owner; you are a creditor. The borrower pledges to pay you a specified amount of interest on specified dates, generally twice a year, and to repay the principal on the date of maturity stated on the bond.

The bond may mature 10 years from now, but you are free to sell it on the open market at any time at the currently quoted price. You would, of course, lose if the price at the time you sold was below your purchase price. The company's commitment to pay the face value of the bond is on the day it comes due.

Your income from the bond is not affected by any change in interest rates. The issuing company pays the stated rate of interest until maturity. If interest rates decline, however, and the issuer is able to replace your loan at a lower interest cost, your bond may be called in and paid off before maturity.

Some bonds mature in a few months or years. These are short-term issues. Others mature after many years and are called long-term issues. They are normally issued in units of $1,000 par value. Bonds usually have two rates of interest; a stated rate and an effective rate. The stated rate, called the coupon or nominal rate, is printed on the bond. The effective rate depends upon the price you paid for the bond. If you pay less than the bond's par value, the effective rate is higher than the bond's coupon rate; if you pay more than par, your effective rate is less than the coupon rate.

Marketability or liquidity (the ease with which you can convert your bonds into cash) is also important. If your bonds are bought and sold frequently, it is likely that you can get a fair price if you should have to sell in a hurry. If your bonds are in bearer form, there are fewer restrictions on their sale when you want to sell before maturity. But, because bearer bonds are vulnerable to theft, they must be kept in a safe-deposit box. Registered bonds are safer since payment of principal and interest will be made only to the registered owner.

What bonds should you buy? If the objective is a high degree of liquidity - meaning you may need your cash at a sudden notice - you should invest in top-grade, short-term bonds. If the objective is a steady income plus relative price stability, you may invest in high-to-medium-grade bonds with longer maturities.

Bonds with the highest yield may not be the safest investment. Higher yield generally means greater risk. For example, government bonds find willing buyers even though they carry relatively low interest rates. Bonds of new or unstable corporations are more speculative and the corporations must pay a high return to attract investors.

You should always be interested in the maturity date of the bond (that is, the year when the borrower has promised to repay the money borrowed). Long-term bonds generally have higher yields than short-term bonds. There are three main reasons: (1) A distant maturity date makes it difficult to predict the financial strength of the borrower at the time the bonds will fall due. This uncertainty makes it necessary to offer some bonds at a higher yield. (2) In times of high inflation, long-term bonds are a greater risk than short-term issues. If the inflationary trend continues out of control, it could cut deep into the purchasing power of the proceeds by the time the bond matures. (3) When interest rates are on the rise, investors are unwilling to tie up funds in long-term, low-yield bonds. Issuers of long-term bonds must offer higher rates to attract buyers.

Municipal bonds. The tax status of the bond is an important feature. Interest from corporate bonds is taxable. But income from state or municipal government bonds is exempt from Federal tax, which makes them particularly appealing to people in the higher income tax brackets. The tax exempt status of municipals has been questioned, and attempts may be made to alter it through changes in the tax law. It is unlikely, however, that the status of outstanding municipals would be affected.

There are two types of municipal bonds: general obligation bonds, which are backed by the "full faith and credit" of the issuing government, and revenue bonds, which are backed by the charges or tolls of the facility, e.g. turnpike, bridge, or tunnel financed by the bonds. General obligation bonds are the safer investment. While the interest paid on municipals is exempt from Federal income tax and from state income taxes in the state where issued, the interest may be subject to tax in other states. If a municipal bond is purchased at a discount and held to maturity or sold at a profit, the gain attributable to the discount is not tax exempt. It is taxed as a capital gain.

Confidence in state and city bonds today is not what it was in years past, and the prospective investor should not buy blindly. Aspects to be considered are the laws governing any particular bond. Would it be a first debt of an issuing community to be paid? What about the budget of the issuing community? If there is a chronic deficit and the community is in constant need of raising revenue, its bonds might be questionable. On the other hand, if a community keeps a balance between payment on maturing bonds and issuing of new ones, more stability can be inferred. Is this a declining community, one where higher-income people are leaving and lower income people moving in? Look for better balance before buying here. The property tax load is considered significant, too. When heavy, and collections fall below 92 percent, the bond holder may feel nervous about his money - because he is paid from this source.

Most municipal bonds will need the protection of a safe-deposit box, being in bearer form. The holder must watch dates of interest payments and when bonds may be called by the issuer.

Municipal bonds can be bought through a broker; some specialize in this type of investment. You can also turn to mutual funds and unit investment trusts, further discussed below, which will give the same tax advantages without some of the responsibilities attached to individual buying and ownership of municipals.

Stock Market Risks

You do not invest in the stock market as such, you invest in particular companies. There is no guarantee that the companies in which you invest will meet your investment objectives. The stock of the largest companies, as well as of lesser ones, has been known to fall out of favor and succumb to price erosion. When dealing with stocks you must keep in mind that it is impossible to avoid risk even in the seemingly safest of situations. Day-to-day fluctuations in the market or in the price of an individual stock are almost impossible to predict. These are only a few of the hazards of stock ownership, which cannot be stressed too strongly to the novice investor.

Unfortunately, there is no way to eliminate investment risk; no reliable means have been found to predict future economic trends. You must be prepared to see the value of your stock decline as well as rise. During critical periods, the atmosphere surrounding stock market investment is charged with fear and apprehension. Panic selling may take place, sending stock prices down sharply. A potential investor must consider his own emotional makeup. If he cannot operate under conditions of stress, then the stock market may not be for him.

The stock market, a highly complex field, demands patient study. Few stocks, if any, are so safe that they can be forgotten in the vault by the buyer. You can only minimize risk by a constant supervision of your investments. Also, get the best advice you can.

If you have a broker who has satisfied you in the past, rely on his judgment. If you have had no experience in security investment, read the literature published by the large investment houses and choose a broker you feel will best serve your purposes.

Can You Afford Stock Market Risk?

Before you start planning an investment program, you must decide how much of a cash reserve you will need to fall back on for emergencies and current obligations. One suggestion: This reserve might approximate the total of your living costs for one year, overhead costs, and any other known obligations, plus an extra 10 percent, *less* insurance benefits and other supplemental income. Such a reserve would be in savings accounts, or in easily converted investments such as government bonds.

Of course, this yardstick may not cover your particular requirements. Just as you had to evolve your own budget to meet your individual circumstances, you will have to take into consideration your needs and concerns before you can decide how much you can afford to invest. Your answers to the following questions will guide you.

1. Have you income from other sources or will your investments be a major source of your funds for day-to-day living?
2. What is your need for the cash you are investing? Can you afford to keep it invested indefinitely? You may need the money at a fixed time, in which case you must restrict yourself to safe and marketable securities which can generally be converted to cash at any time.

If you plan to buy a house or furniture or an automobile on the installment plan, you have specified debts that must be met by specified dates. You should keep funds in the savings bank to meet these obligations as they arise.

Only when you have commitments fully covered and a sound savings bank account should you enter into stock market investment. The person who cannot afford loss should not venture.

What Type of Investor Are You?

In your investment planning, consider your goals and decide how they may be achieved. First, ask yourself if you would be a conservative or long-term investor? An aggressive investor? A speculator? While each of these basic types of investor will measure safety against the risks involved in any investment, they will differ considerably in taking risks.

The conservative or long-term investor holds securities for a long time, seeks steady income together with long-term appreciation, and is more interested in safety of principal than anything else. He (or she) must minimize danger of capital loss by avoiding investment which carries higher risk.

The aggressive investor is more venturesome. He buys and sells more often and typically invests in securities bearing the label "businessman risk." He is willing to take more chances in seeking greater capital growth. He is willing to sacrifice some current return, accepting average or below-average income in the expectation of receiving greater return in the years to come.

The speculator often trades in and out for quick profits. He may buy securities with high risk of loss. Speculators are usually knowledgeable and sophisticated. Newcomers to the stock market should avoid speculative issues.

The safe investment which promises some capital appreciation but only over the long term will have investment appeal to the conservative investor but not to the speculator primarily concerned with quick profits. Regardless of investment goals, however, there is no hard-and-fast rule which requires that all funds be maintained in one type of security. For instance, the conservative investor might have the bulk of his funds in investments offering a high degree of safety, a portion in businessman risk investments, and even a small amount in a particular speculation. In other words, at any one time, an investor may have funds in different securities with different safety-risk factors, although the bulk of his funds will be invested in the type of security which best meets his investment goal.

Changes in circumstances may require changes in investment goals. A young person with no family responsibilities may be in the position to speculate. After marriage and assumption of new responsibilities, he may become more conservative. Again, a middle-aged investor must consider the number of years remaining before retirement - when he must look to his investments for retirement capital. An investor who finds that his earnings are rising will be in a higher tax bracket; investments suitable to a lower-bracket investor may not be suitable to one who is taxed at higher rates.

Fixing Your Investment Objectives

Before selecting the securities you buy, you must also decide what you want and need from your investments. Do you want stock that will return dividends every few months and that will be relatively stable in price and high quality? Do you want a high income security in the hope that the income may cover part of your living expenses? Is your objective the sale of the stock at a substantially higher price than what you paid for it? Are you mainly concerned with liquidity and marketability, because you will need cash suddenly for some business or personal purpose and you want to be sure you can turn in the issue at a price approximating your cost whenever the need arises?

If your objective is "trading" profits, you will generally have to deal in stocks that are fairly risky and which fluctuate widely in price. If liquidity is your aim, you will have to buy stocks of the highest grade that fluctuate only slightly in price. High income, high profits, high stability, and high liquidity do not come in one package.

Decide on your objective or objectives. As a guide, here are some suggestions to consider:

1. For investment, choose sound, essential industries. Food and utilities are basic industries and can more readily hold their values during economic declines than nonessential industries that provide services and luxuries. Of course, all essential industries must be watched and attention paid to any trend that might suggest a particular industry is becoming replaced or outmoded by new technological developments.

2. Invest in companies that are recognized leaders in their

industries. True, some analysts do not agree with this advice and hold that the only substantial profits are made in new, unknown companies. But you are investing, not trying to "get rich quick." Some smaller companies may turn out to be more profitable than well-known firms; the chance of choosing such a company is often a matter of luck. The advantages in selecting the recognized companies is that they have proven their ability, their management is experienced, they will have resources for research, and can finance their needs more easily than smaller companies.

3. Invest in several different companies, each in a different industry. Over a period of time you undoubtedly will make a bad investment. If you invest in only one company, an error may be costly; if you have, say, six different stocks, your good judgment on four of them may more than offset a bad decision on one or two. Of course, you may also "hedge" in the same way by investing in mutual funds.

4. Invest about the same amount in the shares of each company you select. Do not make a favorite of any one stock. There are many sound industries.

5. Invest in shares listed on a major securities exchange, preferably the New York Stock Exchange. Before its stock may be listed on a major exchange, a company must file information with both the private financial authorities and the Federal government. Specific standards must be met; regular reports must be published; transactions are under the constant check of the exchange, the Federal government, the Securities and Exchange Commission (SEC) and expert investors and bankers. Furthermore, a listing on the exchange makes it easier to buy or sell stock. Listing, of course, is no guarantee of merit, but it is a likely indication that the company will operate according to current business standards.

6. Invest in shares that can show an unbroken earnings or a dividend record or both for the last 10 years. Such a record indicates that an enterprise is sound.

7. Buy shares that over the past 10 years have earned at least 5 dollars for every 4 paid out in dividends. A company should not pay out all it earns, but should build up a reserve to

handle emergencies or to insure its ability to take advantage of future opportunities. A company that earns considerably more than its dividend is preferred to one that just about earns it.

8. During a period of a year or two, sell at least one stock, choosing the weakest on your list without considering the original cost. Invest the proceeds in a more profitable security.

9. Choose an established brokerage firm. When you place an order to buy or sell, do not set a fixed price; buy or sell "at the market." Buying or selling at the market means your order will be filled at about the price of the next transaction in your stock on the exchange. This is a better approach than giving your broker a fixed price. You are a long-term investor, and even an expert cannot fix the value of a stock to within fractions of a point. Since you are investing for the long term, it will be completely unimportant over that period whether you paid $20 or $21 for a specific share of stock.

10. Do not buy on margin. The cost of borrowing from your broker and putting up stock as collateral is not only high in terms of interest, but risky as well. If the price of the stock falls, the broker will demand either more money or the sale of the stock—at a loss.

11. If you do buy on margin, you should check the fine print of your agreement and understand the rights retained by your broker. You may find you have to notify him if you want to prevent his taking certain buy-and-sell actions. The broker wants to save paperwork; his rights may not always suit your plans.

12. Brokers find it easier to hold the stock of small investors "in street name." You may prefer to insist that your stock is registered in your name. Customers are now insured to $100,000 against brokerage house insolvency. If you deal with more than one house, or husband and wife maintain separate and joint accounts with one broker, the insurance is $100,000 for each account. Some brokerage houses offer additional insurance protection against the loss of securities and cash in their keeping. There is, of course, no insurance against stock market loss.

Broker Services and Costs

May 1, 1975 marked the end of fixed brokers' fees. Congress ordered the brokerage community to "cease and desist" the practice of fixing commission rates. In theory, at least, there would be free competition for investment business. In practice, the large institutional investors were chief beneficiaries. The new small investor looking for a broker will want to check around, inquire of friends, and find out what services are offered by particular brokerage houses. The large firms often have package deals which may or may not suit you. Fees may be advantageous.

If a newcomer to the market, you may want skillful advice and feel the broker's fee well worthwhile.

Discount brokers. The discount brokers who came on the scene several years ago and have been proliferating ever since are primarily for the seasoned investor since they offer "no frills" service. Generally, according to one leading discount house, the average customer is well-heeled and has a stock portfolio in the $50,000 range.

For the investor looking for execution of his order only, the discounter can offer substantial savings in commissions. As the newcomer gains market experience, he or she can obtain current rates from discount houses and consider if it is time to act without advice in order to achieve substantial savings.

A recent trend has been for some discounters to offer some frills and for some prestige full-service brokers to compete with discounters on commissions and to offer services, too.

When to Buy Stocks

A review of the stock market's history indicates that there is a cyclical character to prices. The trouble, however, is that the low and high markets stand out clearly only in retrospect on charts which show "where the market has been," not necessarily where it is going. True, the expert studies the current market to determine whether it is advisable to buy or sell at current market prices and to predict the future moves of a particular stock. But for the average investor, market analysts suggest, "Give up any idea of beating the market." The retiree, in particular, will want to develop a conservative investment program.

If appropriate to your circumstances, you can use such approaches as dollar cost-averaging or a plan put out by a brokerage house.

Dollar cost averaging. In a dollar cost-averaging program you periodically invest a fixed amount in the same stock (every month or quarter). Your money buys more shares when prices are low and fewer when prices are high. However, if the price is on a down cycle, you are merely buying an increasing number of shares of a declining stock. If the stock price is on the upswing, buying during the temporary decline lowers the average price of your holdings, thereby increasing the potential gain, assuming the stock goes up again. Of course, if you have to unload the stock during a bearish market, you will come out a loser. To be sure, if you could have afforded to keep buying the low-cost shares you might later have made a profit. The possibility also exists that the stock will go up. Company bankruptcies are also a risk.

Regular investment plans. If you are a new investor interested in a plan for gradual investments on a budget, you can obtain such planning information at the New York Stock Exchange which lists member firms offering such plans.

Information About Investments

To reduce the element of risk, familiarize yourself with services available to the investor. Here are sources of important data on investing:

1. The Department of Public Information, New York Stock Exchange, 11 Wall Street, New York 10005. You may write for a list of member firms which will guide you to brokers who will handle your type of account. The office will give general information helpful to the small investor and to the newcomer to the stock market. Inquire about the "Investor's Kit," a useful compendium of elementary information, available at low cost.

2. The financial sections of newspapers and the publications of concerns specializing in financial developments. Several

long-established, respected financial services operate throughout the country; they summarize basic news. These are available to any subscriber in any town or city. Many libraries have in their reference rooms copies of *The Wall Street Journal, The New York Times, Barron's, Forbes,* and other periodicals giving financial news.

3. The companies themselves. If you write to a company whose stock you may be interested in buying, you can obtain an annual report and prospectus which will give you information about the company.

4. The officers of a bank in your locality. Banks generally employ security experts to help guide their customers in investments. If you go to an officer in your bank and tell him your investment needs and objectives, you can usually obtain advice. Large banks will act as agents in certain transactions involving the purchase and safekeeping of different types of securities. Charges, however, should be compared with those made by brokerage houses as they tend to be considerably higher.

5. Stockbrokers. Many brokerage firms maintain large research departments and many have branches throughout the country. They can provide a valuable source of information.

6. Investment advisory services. Unless you are a substantial investor, they are probably not for you. Their fees are considerable for their weekly and monthly reports.

7. Investment counsel firms. These firms charge fixed fees for their advice and are prepared to manage a client's complete investment portfolio. The larger firms usually do not accept clients with small accounts. Fees are in keeping with the means of substantial clients.

8. Most bonds are publicly rated by well-known financial and advisory services, such as Moody's or Standard & Poor's. You may get these ratings at your bank or at a large library.

Investing in Mutual Funds

The emphasis in the previous pages was on your personal planning and execution of an investment program. If you feel you have not the time, ability, or temperament for such a program, you might consider mutual funds where management takes care of the investments. Even if you have a securities investment program, you may want to diversify by putting some of your capital into the funds.

Since mutual funds differ widely in objectives and in return to investors, you will want to analyze the opportunities they offer and decide on those best suited to your investment goals. The fact that a fund has professional management is no guarantee of success. There are mutuals that do well for their investors, some that just get by and others that are dismal failures. As is true in considering any investment, you must exercise judgment. You may want to delegate some one to do some of your investment thinking, but you should not surrender your overall investment judgment responsibility.

The idea behind mutual funds is practical. The investment capital of many investors, large and small, goes into a professionally managed fund which then invests to common stock, preferred stock, bonds, or specialized investments such as gold funds, convertible bonds, convertible preferred stock, real estate ventures, or foreign companies. There are also money market funds and tax-exempt municipal bond funds. New types of mutual funds will continue to appear.

There are two basic types of mutual funds: Closed end and open end. Closed-end funds issue a specific number of shares when formed and, since they do not intend to issue more, are "closed-end." Shares are traded on the stock exchange or over the counter and in buying or selling you act through a broker as you do in common stock transactions. Closed-end shares currently do not appeal to the general investor.

An open-end company is called "open-end" because its capitalization is open. Such companies create and sell shares whenever you want them, buy them back and retire the shares whenever you want to cash in your chips. In other words, you join by turning over your funds to the company and getting newly created shares which represent your pro rata share of the entire fund.

Today, the term "mutual funds" generally applies to open-end companies, and the main discussion in the chapter applies to open end funds.

Open-end mutual funds vary in the type of investment and risks. The prospectus of each fund will identify its objective: Here are some of the types of funds available.

Growth funds. The objective of these funds is to achieve growth in the value of shares, which eventually leads to growth in income. Dividend return tends to be low, because these funds are intended for the long-term investor who looks for capital appreciation. Growth fund assets are usually invested in common stock up to about 90 percent. There are a number of types among growth funds, some of which carry a higher risk than others. Also available are funds aimed at long-term capital growth which have a good record of performance.

Income funds. Investments here are primarily in high-yield securities, mainly corporate stocks and bonds. There are differences within this category, as some income funds will take risks in order to give shareholders a higher yield. Conservative investors, particularly older individuals looking for income turn to these funds.

Growth and income funds. Combining investments in stocks and bonds, these funds endeavor to give shareholders both high dividends and growth.

Because so many mutual funds are in "families," shareholders in one type of fund within the family can switch to other types easily; also, it is no longer difficult to switch to a competing fund. A modest fee may be charged for group transfers or there may be no charge.

Most mutual funds pay quarterly dividends each year; some pay semi-annually. The amounts will vary depending on fund earnings. The fund receives return on its investments and members' shares are distributed proportionate to holdings, after management fees and operating expenses are deducted. In addition, capital gains distributions resulting from profitable security sales by the fund may be made to shareholders. If desired, funds reinvest shareholders' dividends and capital gains and thus increase the investment. Mutual fund shares can be redeemed at any time.

Buying Mutual Funds

Open end mutual funds are bought either through brokerage offices or selling organizations in the case of "load" funds, and directly from the fund in the case of "no loads." The terms refer to sales charges or the lack of them as explained below.

If you refer to the mutual fund listing in the financial pages of *The Wall Street Journal*, for example, you will find a listing with such entries as:

	NAV	Offer Price	NAV. Chg.
Fund X	19.84	N.L. +	.10
Fund Y	11.79	12.64	.03

NAV, as explained above the listing, stands for net asset value per share. The offering price includes net asset value plus maximum sales charge, if any. An entry listed N.L. means that there is no sales charge. An increasing number of funds are no-loads. At one time, load funds were represented as superior in management to no-loads, but the record of no-loads in recent years indicates that this is not necessarily so. There are superior loads and superior no-loads; both types are vulnerable to poor records. Therefore, in choosing a fund, you look to the type of fund you want and its record, not to charges or lack of them. Obviously, many investors prefer to avoid sales charges where they can find a fund to their liking; this explains the number of funds now available under the no-load category. You will note from the listings that many fund families will offer both types.

While no-loads are generally handled direct by mail, some brokerage houses may handle them.

You can buy mutual funds by making a large single investment or you can invest fixed amounts over a period. A minimum investment will be required in any case. Where there is a load, or sales charge, your investment will be diminished by this commission, generally in excess of 8 percent. In the case of the no-loads, all your investment goes to work in the fund. It should be noted that both types of funds charge an annual management fee. Look also, before you invest, for other charges such as redemption fees. The fund's prospectus will alert you. You will have to ask yourself if investing in funds where charges run high is justified in terms of their record.

An open-end fund will redeem your shares at your request for the net asset value of the fund, which approximates the market value of all the securities owned by the fund divided by the number of shares. As market prices vary each day the net asset value fluctuates.

Money Market Funds

With the volatile upward movement of interest rates on the short-term money market and the decline and uncertainty of stock prices, money market funds first appeared around early 1973, attracting cash seeking temporary shelter and high return. When interest rates plummeted, money market funds suffered a period of decline and then boomed when interest rates rose in 1978. In considering money market funds, periods of rise and decline should be expected. Even at low ebb, money market funds serve a purpose for those who want a handy parking place for cash which is to be switched quickly at an opportune moment to the stock market or other investments.

Money market funds are regarded as low risk investments; the fund invests in a diversified list of short term money market instruments. Some funds concentrate heavily on one type or another, others carry portfolios of varying percentages of short-term obligations. Investments are made in Treasury bills and other securities issued by the United States government and its agencies, bank certificates of deposit, high grade commercial paper, letters of credit, and other short-term debt securities. There are even funds which invest only in short-term tax exempts.

The money market funds advertise widely. By using a mail-in coupon from one of the advertisements appearing particularly in financial pages or newspapers and journals, you can secure a prospectus which will list all charges and expenses, and other information.

Money market funds will differ on minimum initial investment;

$1,000, $2,500, $3,000 are often asked. They are listed among other mutual funds, under the "family" heading when they are part of such a group. The Net Asset Value (NAV) is stated as $1 and often followed by N.L. for no-load. But a fund might have a monthly maintenance charge which would weigh more heavily against a small account than a large one.

Gains and losses are generally not realized in money-market funds. Shares are redeemed for exactly what you paid, plus accrued interest. A money-market fund may allow you to write checks for $500 or more on your fund account. This may be an advantage. Your money continues to earn interest until the check clears which may be days after you have made out the check.

Tax-Exempt Municipal Bond Funds and Unit Investment Trusts

Tax-exempt municipal bond funds. These funds invest in municipal bonds of varied ratings. The prospective investor will want to be satisfied with a fund's portfolio as described in its prospectus. One fund may be fully invested in bonds rated A or better, another may place a proportion of investment in Baa bonds, another may have a more speculative portfolio, say, bonds rated below BBB or Baa. A fund with substantial assets in the riskier bonds will offer higher yields in compensation. A fund does not remain static; the function of management is to move with market conditions; moreover, redemptions must be financed. To keep both asset value and yield high is the aim; even the best management will miss under pressure of unfavorable conditions. Generally speaking, municipals have, over the years, been considered low-risk investments. But the potential investor and the current investor must consider economic conditions and trends and other factors which might affect municipals.

Most tax-exempt bond funds offer the same types of flexibility possible in other types of mutual funds. You may receive your dividends regularly or have them reinvested—for tax-free compounding. You may have a systematic payout plan, if you wish—particularly useful at retirement. If in a fund family, you may switch to another type of fund for a low-cost transfer fee. Some funds may offer special features, such as free check-writing, as in the money market funds (generally, $500 minimum), and the privilege of redeeming shares by phone or wire.

Redemptions are at net asset value—which may be more or less at the time of share purchase.

When you invest directly in a no-load tax-exempt municipal bond fund, there are no sales charges. However, load funds are obtainable from brokers. Management fees are charged by all the funds; many are below 1 percent. Minimum investments vary: $1,000, $2,500, $5,000 are common.

Unit investment trusts. Here, you buy into a portfolio of specific bonds with a set maturity date, but you may redeem units at any time without fee or penalty. While you do not have fees for management since none is required for a set portfolio, you may have a modest administrative charge and a not so small front-end load sales charge. Sales charges, of course, diminish the amount of your investment. Units in multiples of $1,000 may be acquired. Frequently, $5,000 is the minimum.

Sales charges or not, the unit investment trusts have more than held their own against the newcomer tax-exempt bond funds, and have maintained their lead. Asset values of unit trusts can drop, but over the long term, investors can receive more income than from the funds. At a favorable investment period, you can seize upon the high tax-free yields. If you find yourself receiving a lower return than is currently obtainable, you might opt out in favor of higher paying units obtainable at that time. Usually, a trust will buy back units, the seller receiving current asset value which may be more or less than paid. When you sell at a loss, you have a tax deduction. Gain, of course, if taxed.

Unit investments trusts are put together by major brokerage houses. Like the tax-exempt municipal bond funds, trusts are available in the bonds of various states and also those of specific states. A trust may mature in, say, 15 years, or last over 40 years; there are also shorter term trusts available. Other types of unit trusts, often short term, are also offered outside the area of tax exempts.

Understand the marketplace. All new investors in municipal bonds, whether by personal investment or through funds and trusts, should understand that when interest rates rise, prices decline. Thus, principal can be eroded. But much investment in bonds, all types, is for the long-term, and in the past has proven a useful, conservative-type producer of income. Today, all investors have to be wary, and watchful of their interests. The patterns of the past are not constant.

Information on Mutual Funds

Mutual fund data is readily available. The public information center for the industry is the Investment Company Institute, 1775 K Street, N.W., Washington, D.C. 20006. Many no-load funds are represented by the No-Load Mutual Fund Association, Valley Forge, Pennsylvania 19481.

Also seek out the *Mutual Fund Directory*, published by the Investment Dealers' Digest, 150 Broadway, New York, New York 10038; *Pocket Summary of Mutual Funds*, from Kalb Voorhis & Company, 726 Woodward Building, Washington, D.C. 20005; Johnson's Investment Company's *Charts*, Rand Building, Buffalo, New York 14203; information from Arthur Lipper Corp., 176 Broadway, New York, New York 10038. *Forbes Magazine*, 60 Fifth Avenue, New York, New York 10011, publishes special annual issues on mutual funds.

A useful and informative monthly publication is *Fundscope*, Suite 700, 1900 Avenue of the Stars, Los Angeles, California 90067. The April issue each year is a comprehensive guide to mutual funds and their performance. This magazine does not sell funds but aims to state the facts concerning them for the guidance of investors.

The records of the closed-end companies are found in all the standard manuals. Most of them are traded on the stock exchanges and their day-to-day price fluctuations are easily followed in such publications as *The Wall Street Journal*, *The New York Times*, other city newspapers and *Barron's*. Large libraries are likely to have *Investment Companies*, data published annually by Wiesenberger Services Inc., 1 New York Plaza, New York, New York 10004. Where material is unavailable at a library, check stockbrokers' offices.

Study the stock market quotations on mutual funds which are

carried daily in many newspapers. While the past record of many funds has generally been good, like other investments they have slipped in bear markets. The newcomer to mutual fund investment has no guarantee that the funds that have consistently made a good showing will do so in the future, but he can avoid the more showy and speculative funds that tend to zoom and fizzle.

The funds themselves will, of course, be happy to mail you their literature. A broker will advise you. Through your reading and inquiries, you can enlarge your understanding of mutual funds so that, in deciding to buy, you do so from an informed background.

CHAPTER 6

Your Life Insurance Program

You should buy insurance with caution. Consider life insurance only if you feel a responsibility to others who will suffer financially in case of your death. Estimate your dependents' needs and whether you can afford a policy that will meet these needs. Do this before shopping for a policy so that you have at least a clear perspective of your insurance requirements before you tackle the complications of various insurance packages and the pressure of an insurance agent. Don't play a passive role and let yourself be selected as a "prospect" by a neighborhood insurance representative; by a relative who has recently become an insurance agent or broker; or by a company advertisement which has hooked you into coupon-signing without too much - or any - forethought.

In the following pages, we will try to guide you on how to estimate your insurance requirements and how to select a policy among the many in the marketplace.

How Much Insurance Do You Need?

Although you will not know the true answer, because the actual date of death is unknown and even the fatally ill have been known to outwit the prognosticators, it is well to sit down with paper and pencil to do some very hard, cold figuring. You can assess your needs only by asking just where would the family stand if you died now?

A realistic appraisal calls for drawing up two columns, for liabilities and assets. To begin with liabilities, your family would first face the high cost of death. Ask yourself how you stand on medical hospitalization insurance in case of prolonged illness or injury prior to death. Would the house be sold? Could your wife earn a salary? How long would your children be dependent?

Consider the funeral arrangements. Do you have a cemetery lot? Would the family have to purchase one or have you stated a preference for cremation? Common sense, not morbidity, dictates that you investigate and make decisions on final arrangements.

Where would your family stand financially once the costs of illness and death were paid? In your estimates, you can only use current figures. A net worth tabulation will help you here. You can write down the state of your assets, including any company or organization benefits payable at death, and also the family indebtedness.

From your budgeting experience, you know basically what it would cost your dependents to live month by month. (For convenience, use a monthly basis in your calculations.) In so many years, some members of your family are likely to be self-supporting, but you may also have to reckon that others, because of incapacity or declining years, may not be. Write down as close an estimate as possible of your financial commitment. For example, a son, already a capable teenager, might be able to earn through his college years and only need your support for another 5 years. But the contribution you make toward the care of an incapacitated brother might go on for 25 years.

Consider the benefits available for your wife and family from Social Security. (Obtain a current record of your credits which will come with information on obtaining a provisional working figure for your present purpose.) You have to cover the anticipated short-fall either through your own assets or through insurance. Essentially, your calculations should take into account these areas exposed by your death:

Last expenses. Cash should be easily available in a joint savings account.

After-death period. If you can keep about half a year's income in savings you can provide adequately for the readjustment your family would be making.

The home. If you are repaying a mortgage, use insurance to cover it.

Income for living expenses. In general, this is the main area to be covered by life insurance policies by the breadwinner who does not have other very substantial assets.

Education of children. You will use insurance, but the family will have to fend for itself, too.

Your wife. If you have children, your widow would receive Social Security benefits until each child reaches the age of 18. A child who is a full-time student receives benefits through the 21st year. During the so-called "blackout" period, your widow would not be entitled to benefits on your Social Security record until reaching the age of 60. To cover her lifetime income needs through insurance would be exceedingly expensive. A wife's best insurance is her ability to earn for herself in case of necessity. Where this would not be possible, try to build up her assets such as investments.

Total up the sum of financial needs listed on estimate sheets and compare this with the total of estimated benefits to be paid by Social Security and other sources and estimated income from sources within the dependent's control. If there is a deficit, you will then have a specific amount which insurance may cover. Even if there is no deficit, you may consider insurance as a cushion to meet unforeseen events and inflation.

Finally, review your insurance needs every few years or at any time there is a change in your family or economic condition.

Shopping For Insurance

The insurance industry has spent millions of dollars selling itself as an institutional friend of the American public. Don't be lulled by its appeals to hearth and family. Insurance companies sell insurance to make money and have devised policies which tend to give them the investment edge. Generally, these are permanent type policies financed by premiums part of which are actually a "savings" deposit building up a cash surrender value. If you want to save you may be wiser to do your own saving, seeking the best current investment rates which insurance companies generally cannot match.

Term Insurance

For pure insurance protection, the first type of policy you should consider is term insurance which has no cash value buildup, and, for the lowest rates, you should look to low-cost group policies offered by an association you belong to, and, if you live in a state which allows such plans, savings bank insurance.

The cost of term insurance is easy to price and compare. Premium costs are listed for age and amount - and you merely have to compare the premium rates offered by each insurer. Term insurance offers coverage for a specific span of time, covering either a certain span of years, one, two, or five years or up to a certain age. Usually, term policies do not go beyond age 70.

Costs should not be the only criterion; you want to check on your right to renew in case of disability and perhaps options to convert to permanent insurance.

Renewable term insurance is preferred; renewal rates are stated and guaranteed, even though rates may rise in the meantime, and you do not have to produce evidence of *insurability* as you renew for a new term. Even if your health fails, you can still renew your policy.

If your preference is for straight life, but you cannot presently afford it, make sure that your term policy is *convertible*. This means that, still without giving evidence of insurability, you may convert to a straight life or endowment policy. However, you may have to inform the company that you intend to convert, and the policy may have a deadline for doing so. Be sure to check on this point. If you have 10-year term insurance, for instance, you may have to announce an intention to convert before the first 7 years have elapsed.

Term insurance may be used in addition to whole life insurance when you have extra risks to cover at certain times. Also a decreasing term policy may help meet a mortgage debt in case of death. As the amount of the debt and the consequent financial responsibility decreases so does the amount of the policy.

When you enter into a life insurance policy program based solely on term policies, do not forget to consider that your term premium rates will increase with your age as you renew your term policies. These increased costs should be compared with the cost of permanent insurance. One advantage of permanent insurance is that the premium rate for the policy remains constant and fixed at the age you took out the policy. However, in making a comparison, remember that though term rates increase as you grow older, your family's need for insurance protection also decreases.

Whole Life Insurance

With whole life insurance (also referred to as straight or ordinary life), you pay a certain premium; you receive life coverage and other stated benefits. The age at which you buy your policy fixes the premium rate at which you will continue to pay. Your policy acquires a "cash value" because the company invests part of the premiums. As the cash surrender values increase, the element of pure insurance decreases. The cash value does not increase the face amount of the policy. However, it may be useful in raising loans and can help you to cover your insurance if, at some time or other, you are unable to pay premiums.

If you eventually wish to discontinue premium payments altogether, several possibilities are open to you: You can receive less insurance protection throughout your life (based on the cash value); you can set an ending date to the full protection; you can obtain a cash settlement for your canceled policy; instead of life insurance, you may elect to receive income for a certain period.

Your policy will automatically put some provision into effect if you fail to pay premiums. Check to find out what it is because, if you cannot pay, you may wish a different provision to be made and you will have to so notify the company.

Limited payment life. This policy is actually straight life, but with premiums payable within a stated time, say 20 or 30 years, or by a certain age, such as 65, instead of being payable annually over a whole lifetime. The higher premiums build up cash values faster, but the cost might prove a burden to a young person who will not reach highest earning capacity until middle life. For the person whose early years mark the high earning point (an athlete or actor, for example), a limited payment policy may prove useful. Note that early death after completion of premium payments would make this a very expensive policy.

Combination Policies

Insurance companies offer various types of policies, varying premium payments and coverage at different age periods. A policy may combine permanent with term options. Another policy may offer substantial coverage during the period the insured has young children with a decrease in coverage afterwards. Yet, another policy may start with low initial premiums followed by an increase that will level out after a period of time. To meet competition and changing economic conditions insurance companies have found it profitable and even necessary to come up with variations and combinations of basic insurance policies. You may want to decide on a policy because of the flexibility of these options, but before doing so, check the policy for the returns paid on the investment element of the policy. If it is low, the policy may not be suitable as a low investment return actually increases the cost of the policy.

Family Income

With a separate policy or rider you may obtain term insurance running for a certain period (but not beyond a maximum age limit). If you die during the period of coverage, your beneficiary receives a monthly income from date of your death. If you survive the stated period, the policy pays nothing.

Say your wife is the beneficiary. Depending on the company issuing the policy, there will be a choice of ways in which she could benefit. She might receive your basic policy's benefits immediately with monthly income till the end of the period. She could reserve payment of the main benefit till after the monthly payments had run out. She could split the main benefit, having part paid when the monthly payments start, the rest when they end.

Note that if you take out this type of policy, say, for 10 years, and you live for 9 of them, your beneficiary would receive one year's monthly income. This may be suitable if you are, say, protecting a child who will be able to earn for himself by the time the term expires.

Examine the settlement options of your basic policy and consider if family income protection is more suitable than supplemental term insurance.

The appeal of family income policy is greatest for a husband concerned that, on his premature death, he would be survived by a comparatively young widow with minor children. Policy combines permanent insurance with *decreasing term coverage*. It can provide an extra in the form of monthly income which starts on the death of the insured and continues for a specified period, e.g., 10, 15, or 20 years from the date the policy was originally purchased. Monthly income might be 1 percent per $1,000 permanent insurance (e.g., $10 per $1,000), 2 percent or 3 percent (e.g. $20 or $30 monthly income per $1,000 permanent insurance). At the end of the monthly income period, the face amount of permanent insurance is paid to beneficiary. Note that monthly income is paid only if the insured dies prematurely within the specified period. For instance, assume a man buys a $10,000 20-year family income policy, paying $100 monthly income (i.e. 1 percent of $10,000 face). If he dies one year after purchase, his beneficiary would get $100 a month for 19 years and then $10,000 face. On the other hand, if he lives for 21 years after policy purchase, his beneficiary would not get any monthly income but would receive immediate payment of $10,000 face.

Family Maintenance

This policy is a combination of permanent insurance and level term insurance. Unlike the family income policy, the period over which monthly income payments will be made to the beneficiary starts at time of insured's death, if he dies within specified period. For instance, a husband is 30 years old. He buys 20-year, 1 percent family maintenance policy, $10,000 face. If he dies prior to age 50, his widow-beneficiary will receive $100 a month for 20 years and then payment of $10,000 face. However, if he dies after age 50, there will be no monthly income payments but $10,000 face amount will be paid immediately to the widow.

A portion of each monthly income payment will reflect interest return on permanent insurance part of policy left on deposit. This interest is taxable income to the beneficiary. The remaining portion of each monthly payment will reflect an installment settlement of term coverage, constituting a principal (tax-free) and interest return. The interest portion, though, can be freed from tax—up to $1,000 a year—where the surviving spouse is the beneficiary. A lump-sum payment when monthly income ceases is income tax free.

Family Plan

A family plan policy is combined permanent and term insurance covering all members of the family. The purchase of the family plan policy by younger men continues to increase. This is how such a policy operates. The young father is the primary insured, covered by permanent insurance in the largest amount. His wife and minor children are secondary insureds, covered by term insurance in small amounts. While it is true that secondary beneficiaries normally survive the primary beneficiary, premature deaths do take place. While insurance recovery on the death of a secondary beneficiary is comparatively small, it may provide the funds needed to meet bills resulting from the dependent's last illness or funeral cost. Or if the mother of the family dies, funds are available for child care while adjustments are made to new conditions.

Insurance on wife and children is offered by some companies as a rider to the husband's insurance.

Check what your company issues in this type of life insurance and consider if it is for your family. A common package would be $5,000 whole life protection for the father, and term coverage of $1,000 each on the lives of the mother and children. Variations of the family plan are favorites with the insurance agents who sell them, but do not necessarily offer worthwhile protection in many situations.

Insurance Companies

For your own protection you will want to do business with a well-established company and to avoid those which have yet to prove themselves. However, know that the giants of the insurance industry do not necessarily offer the most reasonably priced insurance. In fact, a small company may offer you a better deal, but you should check on the company's background. Make sure it is not a newcomer with a similar name to one well known.

Basically, there are two types of company, though there is some overlapping. A *stock company* customarily issues nonparticipating policies though some may issue participating policies. With such a nonparticipating policy you do not pay as much as you would for a similar policy issued by a *mutual company* (usually identifiable by the word "mutual" in its title). The company has set the rate of the nonparticipating policy *at what it expects the insurance to cost*. In advance, you know exactly what you will pay for your coverage.

In the case of the participating policy, the company has fixed premium rates *in excess of what it expects the insurance to cost*. Why then should you consider this type of policy? In the long run it may prove less costly than a nonparticipating policy because you will receive dividends after the first 2 or 3 years. The dividends are not taxable; they are refunds on your premiums made when the company's actual operating costs are known. The amount of your annual dividends will, of course, vary with company decision and profit. In prosperous times, your company's participating policy may pay good dividends, but an economic slump might mean small, or even no, dividends.

Company policies differ on payment of dividends, some tending to increase them in the later years, thus benefiting the long-lived, long-paying insured person. If you have a participating policy, you can accept dividends in a number of ways, from cash payment (which would enable you to build your regular savings account) to buying additional insurance. *Be sure dividends are paid to you as you want* and not automatically applied by the company to the purchase of extra insurance you may not need.

Know Your Insurance Agent

Although savings bank life insurance is available in certain states on a come-and-get-it basis, the vast bulk of life insurance is sold by agents who are sometimes employees of a company and may or may not receive a salary in addition to commission. Usually, they are self-employed people and work only for commission. (Bear this factor well in mind and ask yourself if the insurance the agent is advising for you is the protection your family requires, or if it just pays better.)

When you consider the great importance of life insurance to the security of your family, and the amount of money you will invest, you certainly want to be personally satisfied with the individual who will be making far-reaching recommendations to you and to have some background information on him or her.

If you can interview several company representatives and let them suggest certain life insurance planning for you without committing yourself definitely to any one, you will be in a favorable position to judge both the variations on basic policies offered and the agents who describe them to you.

If an agent has been advising and selling to your friends for some years, you know he or she is no fledgling, but if you are dealing with a person unknown to you, find out how long he or she has been in the business. While it may be agreeable to give some young person a start, let him or her practice on the less knowledgeable; you prefer to know that your agent is experienced, at least four to five years as an agent, and if he can add "C.L.U." after his name, you can be assured he is a Chartered Life Underwriter, having successfully completed examinations and other requirements set by the American College of Life Underwriters.

It should be recognized that an agent may be perfectly sincere in recommendations to you, having been well indoctrinated by the company, but what is offered is not necessarily right for you.

Provide your own clear-cut ideas on the insurance you should have.

Cancelling or Switching Existing Policies

If a policy is no longer needed you should cancel; whether you should switch depends on any savings to be made by dropping the old policy for the new one. All things being equal, new insurance will cost you more than the same insurance bought when you were younger. However, in some cases a switch may provide a saving where the old policy pays no dividends but the new policy does. A switch should not be made unless a careful review of net premium costs are made in relation to dividend payments and investment return. Further, proceed with caution where the switch has been touted by an agent who wants you to drop some other company's policy to take his or hers. This unethical gambit, known as "twisting," has resulted in loss for many people who allowed themselves to be persuaded into dropping policies they had for years. If you meet with this ploy, take the opportunity to review thoroughly what your original company offered and, if changes seem justified, see what they can suggest to meet your present needs. Only if careful investigation proves that the agent had a valid point should you let a former policy lapse in favor of a new one.

Your Employer May Help Buy Your Insurance Coverage

Your company may be able to help you get additional protection through a split-dollar insurance plan. Under this type of plan, your employer purchases permanent life insurance on your life. He pays the annual premium to the extent of the yearly increases in the cash surrender value of the policy and you pay only the balance of the premium. At your death, your employer is entitled to part of the proceeds equal to the cash surrender value or any lesser amount equaling the total premiums he paid. You have the right to name a beneficiary to receive the remaining proceeds which, under most policies, is substantial as compared with the employer's share.

You annually report as taxable income an amount equal to the one-year term cost of the declining life insurance protection to which you are entitled less any portion of the premium provided by you. Simplified somewhat, here is how the tax would be figured in one year. Assume the share of the proceeds payable to your beneficiary (face value less cash surrender value) from a $100,000 policy is $77,535. If the term cost of $77,535 insurance provided by the employer is $567, you pay a tax on $567, less your payment of premium. So if you paid a premium of $209, you pay tax on $358. Assume in the fourth year, you pay no premium and the amount payable to your family is $69,625. (Under the split-dollar plan, the benefits payable to your beneficiary continuously decline; the employers share increases annually because of the continued payment of premiums and the increase in the cash surrender value.) The term cost provided by your employer toward $69,625 is $549; you pay tax on the full $549.

Despite the tax cost, you may find the arrangement an inexpensive method of obtaining additional insurance coverage through your employer's help. For example, taking the taxable premium benefit of $549 from the above example, if you are in the 32 percent bracket, the cost of almost $70,000 insurance protection in that year is $175.68 ($549 x 32%).

Group Life

As a member of a union or a professional association, or simply as an employee, you may be able to participate in group life insurance coverage. You may have to contribute to the premium (some employers pay total cost), but your group term insurance will not cost as much as you would pay as an individual. Moreover, there may be no medical examination.

Usually, upon retirement or on leaving a group, the member can convert to individual whole life or endowment, but it will cost usual rates, and at 65, say, these would be extremely high. *Group Paid Up* is a plan which helps to overcome such objections. Your contributions go toward paid up whole life insurance; your employer's go toward term, which covers your life. Upon retirement or leaving the group, you have your paid up whole life insurance which you can use in one of several ways. It can remain in force, or be surrendered for cash or life income. You may also be able to buy additional whole life insurance which will make up for what your employer formerly paid in term coverage.

In few cases will group insurance provide all the protection a family needs, but it can prove a useful addition to other policies and lower the overall cost of life insurance.

In a state offering savings bank insurance, your group may be able to enjoy the advantages of a plan offered to 10 or more employees at low administrative cost.

Savings Bank Insurance

If you live or work in a state where savings bank life insurance is sold, you have an excellent opportunity. These thrift institutions offer advantageous rates. While state law limits the total amount of savings bank life insurance an individual may buy, a broad range of straight life, term, endowments, and many variations can be obtained. All savings bank plans pay dividends, which further reduce the overall cost.

No salesman will call to urge savings bank life insurance upon you; a substantial reason for the low cost is the fact that you must take the initiative, applying for your policy by mail or in person at the bank.

At this writing, New York, Connecticut, and Massachusetts are the only states where the law permits savings bank life insurance. The rules of the system differ in the three states. In New York, savings bank life insurance is available in amounts from $1,000 to $30,000 to residents and those who work in the state. Maximums in Connecticut and Massachusetts are $10,000 and $41,000 respectively. Members of the immediate family, husband, wife, children, parents, brothers, and sisters are also eligible. It is possible that savings banks in other states will be permitted to sell life insurance, also that the amounts may be revised upward to meet today's conditions.

Mail Order Insurance

You may be attracted by an advertisement in which an insurance company in a distant state offers life (or other) insurance. Answering such an advertisement may bring a salesman to your doorstep. Because of the distance, you will have little or no chance of checking on the reliability of the company. Maybe it is sound; maybe the salesman can give good advice, but your best move is to do business nearer home and on a direct basis. Too, you run the danger that the distant company is not licensed to sell in your state. You lose out on the protection your state law may provide, and perhaps open the door to legal complications at your death.

Choosing Your Beneficiaries

You intend the money you are spending annually on life insurance to benefit those financially dependent on you, in most cases, wife and children; sometimes parents. A widowed or divorced career woman may have as much responsibility in this area as a husband or father.

The question is: Have you named your beneficiaries correctly? If not, the people you plan to protect may not derive the benefits you intended. The situation may become particularly involved where divorce is concerned. Perhaps, after a financial settlement has been reached, a former wife and children of the marriage should not benefit from a policy already in force. A change would have to be made in the beneficiaries named.

A point to note here is that when you first take out the policy you should reserve the right to change the beneficiaries. If you do not make this proviso, you must have consent in writing from the person formerly named before the company will make the change.

Your insurance company has a legal staff and if your personal situation is complicated, you should have the agent refer the case to these lawyers. He himself should be able to advise you when no unusual difficulties are involved.

If you are consulting an attorney about your will and estate planning, discuss the question of insurance with him. As the years bring changes, you will undoubtedly find that you must alter the names or order of your life insurance beneficiaries.

Veterans' Insurance

Veterans frequently fail to change the beneficiary's name in their National Service Life Insurance policy. Originally, the insurance may have been intended to benefit parents. Then the serviceman marries, but he neglects to rename his beneficiaries, leaving his widow to find out that she cannot receive the proceeds of the insurance. Renaming beneficiaries of GI insurance is not complicated; consult your local Veterans' Service Agency.

On leaving the service, you should act to replace GI coverage within the 120-day period following discharge. An explanation of policy conversion rights issued by the Veterans Administration is provided for servicemen.

The Decision Is Yours

As we have said, the insurance needs in your family will differ widely from another's. So, too, will your attitude. If you have the resolve to save regularly and put aside the difference between renewable term and ordinary life, you may well find term insurance which covers the years of your greatest financial responsibility to your family to be the answer. In your later years, the need to protect others may have diminished, if not vanished, and you can avoid carrying high-priced coverage. A prudent investment or a savings program can roll up dividends on money that might have gone into cash value insurance.

On the other hand, you may prefer full insurance coverage until you are 65 and, at the same time, you may feel safer with the prospect of the return you will get on the cash value of your policy than with a savings and investment program. Your personal temperament and circumstances will guide your decision.

Finally, when you have decided on a particular policy, you should not sign until you have thoroughly examined all the clauses and made sure that you understand what is contained in the fine print. If the agent from whom you propose to buy the policy will not provide you with a sample copy, go to another agent.

Paying premiums. It will certainly pay you to put money aside regularly to meet your life insurance premiums on an annual basis. If you pay every month, quarter, or half year, you will be liable for the carrying charges leveled for payments on the installment plan.

The Language of Life Insurance

Since the terms used in life insurance are not familiar to all, we give definitions of some below:

Annuitant. A person during whose life an annuity is payable; the recipient of the annuity income.

Annuity. A contract which provides a guaranteed income for a certain number of years or for life.

Beneficiary. The person named in the policy to receive the insurance money upon death of the insured.

Cash value. The money a policyholder will get back if he gives up that policy.

Convertible term insurance. Term insurance giving the insured the right to exchange the policy for permanent insurance without evidence of insurability.

Disability benefits. A rider which provides for waiver of premium, sometimes monthly income also, when the insured is proven totally and permanently disabled.

Dividend. Amount returned to participating policy-holders as a refund of overpaid premiums. It is not taxable; but, being dependent on company operations, it is not guaranteed.

Double indemnity. A policy rider which provides for double the face amount of the policy if death should occur through accident.

Endowment insurance. Payment of a definite sum to a policy-holder, or his beneficiary, after a stated number of years.

Face amount. The sum stated on the face of the policy to be paid on death of the insured or at maturity.

Grace period. The time allowed after the premium due date for payment during which period the policy does not lapse.

Insured. The person on whose life an insurance policy is issued.

Lapsed policy. A policy ended by nonpayment of premiums.

Limited payment life insurance. Whole life insurance paid for in a specified number of years.

Maturity When the policy's face value is payable.

Nonparticipating policy. One that pays no dividends.

Ordinary life insurance, also called straight life, is payable by premiums until death.

Paid up insurance. All premiums have been paid.

Participating policy. Dividends are payable.

Policy. The terms of the insurance contract are set forth on this document which is issued to the insured.

Policy loan. A loan made by the insurance company to a policyholder and secured by the cash value of that policy.

Premium. The regular periodic payment made for the insurance.

Settlement options. Alternative ways in which the insured or beneficiary may have policy benefits paid.

Rider. An endorsement which changes the terms of an existing policy.

Term insurance. A policy payable at death if that event occurs during the term of the insurance.

Waiver of premium. A provision whereby an insurance company will keep a policy in force without payment of premiums. Usually operates as a disability benefit.

Whole life insurance. Includes ordinary or straight life insurance on which premiums are payable until death and limited payment life insurance on which premiums are paid for a certain number of years only.

CHAPTER 7

Planning Ahead for Retirement

Though retirement may lie many years ahead of you, you would do well to start planning for it early so that the after-65 years are free of the cares that beset so many retired people.

Basic living costs have steadily climbed from year to year due to strong inflation. How will matters appear at the end of this century when many a man and woman now in their forties will be retiring? The projection of living costs on page 140 will show you what you will need to maintain your same standard of living 20 years from now.

These figures make uncomfortable reading for the people who will reach retirement age in the early part of the 21st century; and even worse reading for those who will already be retired at that time. We may hope that the projections will prove to be alarmist. Nevertheless, the trend is there: preparation must be made through savings, sound investments, and, where possible, through continued earnings.

Apart from what may occur to retirees in the next century, what about the new or intending retiree at the present time? If inflation were at only 5 percent annually, $1,000 set aside in 1979 would have diminished to $614 of purchasing power in ten years. At 7 percent annual inflation, the $1,000 can buy only about half 1979 value in goods and services. Worse erosion in 1989 is seen at 8

ITEM	% of Budget	Cost	Inflation Rates Constant for 20 Years		
			6%	10%	12%
Housing	20	$2,000	$6,418	$13,457	$19,296
Food	20	2,000	6,418	13,457	19,296
Clothing	15	1,500	4,814	10,093	14,472
Transportation	9	900	2,888	6,056	8,683
Utilities	8	800	2,567	5,383	7,718
Entertainment	8	800	2,567	5,383	7,718
Medical expenses	7	700	2,246	4,710	6,754
Household maintenance	5	500	1,605	3,364	4,824
Savings	5	500	1,605	3,364	4,824
Miscellaneous	3	300	963	2,019	2,894
Total	100	$10,000	$32,091	$67,286	$96,479

percent and 10 percent when the $1,000's buying power is diminished to around $460 and $380.

Of course, at retirement, your budgeting needs will change; some items will diminish while others will increase. Here is a handy checklist of changes you may expect:

Decreased expenses:

Work-related expenses will cease, including, for example, the high cost of commuting to and from work, lunches away from home, and work clothes

Payments to retirement plans will end

Federal income taxes will be lower due to lower taxable income, extra personal exemptions for being 65 or over, tax credit for the elderly, and receipt of nontaxable income such as Social Security, railroad retirement benefits and certain veterans' benefits. But note that you will probably have to budget money for your estimated tax payments as withholding taxes from employment will cease

Mortgage payments may be completed. This would occur for example, where you purchased your house at age 40 on a 25-year mortgage. You would own your house outright at age 65

Savings will no longer be a major budgeting factor since retirement is the time to use your hard saved dollars

You may be entitled to a reduction in property taxes. This break for senior citizens is spreading across the country. Check with your state or county government to see if this benefit is available to you

The overall cost of living may be less if you move from high cost of living areas to within lower cost of living areas, say, from Boston to Miami or Chicago to Atlanta.

Increased expenses:

Medical costs statistically increase with age

Medical insurance, borne by your employer before retirement, will have to be paid by you. Hospitalization under Medicare is free after a minimum payment so your new expense is partially offset

Recreational expenses may increase because of free time available to pursue travel and hobbies, but these increases cannot be generalized; only you know how you will spend your time.

As a rule of thumb, which must be adapted to your particular lifestyle, if your retirement income equals 75 percent of your preretirement income, your retirement will be comfortable; if your retirement income is only 40 percent of pre-retirement income, you are in for a struggle. Make a realistic projection of your needs, then see if your retirement income, discussed below, will be satisfactory.

What Will Your Income Be?

Here are usual sources of retirement income: Social Security; pension from employment or union; profit-sharing plan; individual retirement accounts; retirement plans for self-employed persons; annuity or other insurance payments; investments; interest from savings; United States Savings Bonds; rents; royalties; and personal business.

How many of these sources will you have when you retire? If you are fairly young, you may not have thought much about the subject. You know you will be entitled to Social Security benefits; you may also be relying on a company pension plan. But the declining power of the dollar over recent decades should warn even the young that various sources of income should be developed - the earlier the better.

Your Social Security Benefits

You can roughly figure the amount of your Social Security retirement benefits only if you are not too far from claiming them. Your local Social Security office can supply you with this information. A basic figure is obtained at age 62, with subsequent adjustments for additional years worked. The worker gains 100 percent of benefits by postponing retirement until age 65; increments are given to those working longer. If your spouse will be of retirement age, you should consider your total amount of benefits. But note that even if your spouse worked up until retirement, your benefits will not be double the entitlement of one of you alone. This disparity in the law has come under attack recently and it is hoped that the situation will be remedied by the time you plan to collect.

Developing a Personal Pension Program

Your employer, or prior employers, may have qualified pension or profit-sharing plans under which you may be entitled to benefits when you retire, leave your employer's service, or become disabled. If you die before receiving benefits, your spouse may be entitled to receive benefits. If you are self-employed, you may be able to establish a Keogh plan to provide your own retirement benefits. If you are not covered under any other plan, you may be able to set up an Individual Retirement Account (IRA) to squirrel away funds to be used upon retirement. You need to know your pension rights and opportunities to make a realistic appraisal of what will be available to you when you retire.

Does Your Company Have a Pension or Profit-Sharing Plan?

To prepare for your retirement, you should project the benefits you may expect to receive upon retirement. If they are insufficient, you will have to plan for increased benefits or look to other investments for, retirement income. The federal government, through the tax law, encourages the creation of qualified plans by allowing:

An employer to deduct its contributions to an employee's plan.

An employee to avoid current tax on the contributions made to his account. Tax is not incurred until the employee begins to collect benefits. If certain rules are met, this tax is generally lower than the tax otherwise due on similar amounts.

Tax-free accumulation of income earned on funds invested in the plan.

These benefits apply only to plans which meet technical rules, which generally are aimed at preventing employers from discriminating in their own favor or for certain employee classes and positions. When a plan is approved by the Treasury, it is called a qualified plan.

If you have not already been told, ask your employer or plan administrator what benefits you will receive and at what age or after completion of what period of service they will begin. Benefits may be expressed in several ways. They may be determined actuarily, dependent upon such factors as the amount of contributions, the length of employment, and how successfully the funds were invested. They may be a flat dollar amount for each year of service; for example, your benefit upon retirement may be $10 per month for each year of service. Thus, after 25 years of employment your retirement benefit would be $250 per month. Your benefits may be expressed as a percentage of your average compensation over certain years of service, say 25 percent of your annual salary for the last five years of employment. Thus, if you earned $24,000, $26,300, $29,040, $31,950, $35,150, your annual benefit would be $7,328 (25% of $29,308). Obviously, the closer you are to retirement, the more accurate the estimation of your benefits will be.

You may be permitted or required to make contributions to the plan. Your contributions to an employer plan are not deductible.

Similarly, if amounts are withheld from your pay to make contributions, you must report that withheld amount as current income. But although your contributions are not deductible, there are advantages to contributing. Income earned on your contributions in your employer's plan is not currently taxed to you. Thus your investment may accumulate without current tax costs. Moreover, your money may grow faster by having expert investors handle it. But be forewarned that you could also lose a portion of it. Your contributions are a form of forced savings. If you have difficulty saving, voluntary contributions to your company plan may be advisable.

When you receive your benefits, your contributions are not taxed. Your own contributions also are not subject to forfeiture as are vested benefits derived from employer contributions in the case of death before retirement, if the plan provides for such forfeitures.

What happens if you become disabled prior to retirement? Some plans provide benefits for this contingency. Plans that do provide for payment in such cases usually require proof of total and permanent disability, a minimum age and service requirement (e.g. age 50 with 15 years of service), and a waiting period (e.g. six months) before benefit payments begin. The plan may define what constitutes disability; actual medical proof will be required to sustain a claim of disability. Find out if your plan provides disability benefits and whether such disabilities as mental incompetence, drug addiction, alcoholism, or self-inflicted injury will still entitle you to benefits.

What happens if you die before retirement? If you are covered under a plan to which you make contributions and die before retirement, your contributions must be returned to your estate or beneficiaries whom you have designated. Beyond this, no plan is required to provide any death benefits. However, some plans do.

Plans are allowed to provide that there is a forfeiture of benefits, vested or not, if you die before retirement. However, if you continue to work beyond the age at which you could retire, your benefits will not be lost in the case of death before retirement where a joint or survivor annuity was provided. For example, if your company's normal retirement age is 65 and you continue to work, your joint annuitant will receive benefits should you die thereafter. Learn what death benefits are available and how to proceed in naming a beneficiary.

Death benefits after retirement. If you die after you begin receiving benefits, the type and amount of benefits your estate or beneficiaries will receive will depend in part on the benefits you were receiving prior to death. There may be a modified refund of all your contributions, reduced by amounts already paid out. There may be a guaranteed minimum number of months you are entitled to receive payments after retirement; such payments continue after death. You may be receiving benefits under a joint and survivorship annuity, in which case the annuitant, usually your spouse, will continue to receive benefits for the remainder of the joint annuitant's life.

Plan terminations. If you have been an active participant in a plan and your employer chooses to terminate the plan or, in the case of a profit-sharing or stock bonus plan, to completely discontinue making contributions, you will not lose your benefits to date but you must be prepared to act quickly to avoid immediate taxation.

In general, a lump-sum distribution from a qualified plan is not taxable if, within 60 days from distribution it is reinvested in an individual retirement account, individual retirement annuities or special government bonds or transferred to a qualified plan of your new employer should you change jobs shortly after distribution. If you roll over only part of the distribution, you will be taxed currently on the part not rolled over and that taxable portion will not be subject to special rules permitted for lump-sum distributions. You may not roll over your own contributions to your employer's plan.

Changing jobs. When you leave your present employer before retirement, whether voluntarily or involuntarily, you do not necessarily forfeit your benefits. You look to the vesting schedule of your plan to determine how much of the accrued benefits is yours. The law sets minimum vesting rules. Your plan may vest benefits faster, but in no event will you be entitled to less than 50% after ten years and 100% after 15 years of service.

If your present employer distributes these vested benefits to you in a lump sum, you may roll them over as in the case of plan terminations.

If you do not or cannot roll over the distribution, you are currently taxed on benefits received less the amount of your contributions.

If, when you leave your present employer, you receive no distribution (which is permissible under law), you will not get those benefits until normal retirement age. But you will not get taxed until then. Conversely, if, upon termination of employment, the present value of your benefits is less than $1,750, your employer may distribute cash to you even if you would prefer to leave them until retirement.

How benefits are taxed. Pension benefits, whether payable on retirement in a lump sum or as an annuity are taxable (except for the part representing your own contributions). However, distributions from qualified retirement plans, if in a lump sum, are eligible for special tax rules that will lower the taxation of benefits.

Individual Retirement Accounts (IRA)

If you work and are not covered by qualified or government retirement plans, you may fund your own personal retirement plan, called Individual Retirement Accounts (IRA). There are these advantages to doing so:

1. Investments in an IRA are deductible up to $1,500 or 15% of your pay, whichever is less. If you set up IRA accounts for yourself and a nonworking spouse, you may contribute and deduct up to $1,750 or 15% of your pay, whichever is less. This means that if you are in the 32% bracket and you contribute the maximum to an individual IRA, you would reduce your income tax by $480. Had you merely intended to invest $1,500 of pre-tax income in another type of investment, you would only have had $1,020 after taxes to invest. So, an IRA saves you current taxes and thereby increases the dollars you have to invest.
2. Income earned on funds accumulating in the account is not taxed until the fund is withdrawn.

Counteracting these benefits are several restrictions:
1. You may not start withdrawing from the account until you

reach age 59-1/2 or become disabled. If you do take money out of the account or even borrow using the account as collateral prior to that time, you are subject to a penalty tax.
2. You must start withdrawals by age 70-1/2 to avoid a penalty tax.

What can you expect to accumulate in an IRA? If you are eligible to make the maximum contribution of $1,500 and you make such a contribution every year, this is what you may expect to have on hand at age 65 assuming your funds have been invested in an account earning 8% interest, compounded daily (effective yield 8.45%):

You begin contributions at age	Accumulated funds	You are able to draw out this amount annually for the next 15 years
30	$309,970	$34,315
35	200,362	22,186
40	127,114	14,072
45	78,298	8,670
50	45,764	5,066
55	24,081	2,666
60	9,631	1,066

If your spouse is eligible to establish an IRA, the amount available to both of you may be even more substantial. Of course, all your withdrawals are taxed as ordinary income, but it may well be that your income tax bracket is lower during your retirement years than during your working years so the tax bite may not be as painful.

You may set up your IRA in a number of ways: as an individual retirement account with a bank or brokerage firm, an individual retirement annuity with an insurance company, or with special U.S. Retirement Bonds purchased directly from the Federal Reserve Bank or branch or from the Treasury in denominations of $50, $100, or $500. In deciding which investment form of IRA is for you, the rate of return of your investment should be considered first. Banks have a maximum interest rate, but some banks may be offering less. U.S. retirement bonds have a fixed interest rate of 6%. Annuities may be fixed or variable (no fixed return) or a combination thereof. The fees charged by the institution handling your IRA should be investigated and compared. Typically, savings banks do not charge for establishing or maintaining IRAs. In comparison, insurance companies and brokerage firms do. Furthermore, such charges may be level load, whereby the fees are the same annually, or front load, whereby the fees are heaviest in the early years. However, the imposition of service charges may not be of consequence if the investment yield is greater than the yield offered by institutions which do not charge for services. Another factor to be considered is the method of payment. An IRA annuity will be paid to you in fixed sums monthly, quarterly, or annually. An IRA account may be withdrawn in a lump sum or in any periodic manner (bearing in mind the withdrawal requirements following age 70-1/2 to avoid a penalty tax). U.S. retirement bonds must be redeemed at age 70-1/2 . However, the funds may be rolled over into an IRA account and then withdrawn in amounts conforming to distribution requirements for persons age 70-1/2. IRAs in savings banks are federally insured up to $100,000. After shopping around and considering your needs, select the IRA best suited for you.

Do you have a nonworking spouse? If you are eligible to set up an IRA and your spouse is not working, you may make deductible contributions on your spouse's behalf. The spousal account is subject to the same tax rules and penalties as regular IRAs. The IRAs may be structured in one of two ways. Two separate accounts, one for each spouse, may be established. Alternatively, a single IRA with two subaccounts, one for each spouse, may be created. A joint account is not allowed. However, each spouse may have a right of survivorship in the subaccount of the other.

The maximum deductible contribution is the lesser of 15% of earned income or $1,750 ($875 for each spouse).

Equal contributions to each account are not required, but if you do not make equal contributions, you may lose part of your deduction and be subject to penalties. Where the amounts contributed for each spouse are not equal, the deduction is limited to twice the lower contribution. If for any reason you do not want to contribute to your spouse's account, you may claim a deduction under the regular IRA rule.

Retirement Plans for the Self-Employed

If you are self-employed and have self-employment income from your business or professional practice, you may establish a Keogh (H.R. 10) plan to provide your own retirement benefits. The extent of preferential tax treatment accorded a Keogh plan falls somewhere between a qualified company plan and an IRA. For instance, the amount you may deduct for contributions to a Keogh plan is less than that allowed for a qualified company plan but greater than that allowed for an IRA. Moreover, lump-sum distributions from Keogh plans, like distributions from company plans, may qualify for special averaging provisions; distributions from IRAs are not entitled to such treatment. As in both qualified company plans and IRAs, income earned on contributions to a Keogh plan accumulate tax free and is not subject to tax until funds are withdrawn from the plan.

In deciding if you should set up a Keogh plan, compare (1) an estimate of what a regular investment program would return to you on retirement with (2) an estimate of what the self-employed retirement plan would provide. If your comparison is based on a savings plan at a fixed rate of return, there is no question that the Keogh plan will give a greater return because of the tax benefits provided by the law. However, you should also consider these points before making your decision:

You must include your employees with at least three years of service in your Keogh plan, and contribute funds for their retirement account. However, you deduct your contributions to their account, thus reducing the cost of your contribution. After meeting both your personal and business expenses, do you have cash to put into the fund? You may meet part of this problem by providing that the plan is to have a variable formula of contributions to meet fluctuation in income. The retirement fund is frozen until you reach the age of 59-1/2, become disabled, or die. In case of financial emergency, your use of the fund may subject you to penalty tax.

Each year, you may generally contribute and deduct up to 15% of your earned income, or $7,500, whichever is less. Annual contributions may even be greater than the $7,500/15% limit if you set up a special type of plan, known as a defined benefit or Keogh-plus plan. And, too, you may be able to make voluntary, nondeductible contributions if you allow your employees to make voluntary contributions. However, the additional contribution may not exceed ten percent of earned income, or $2,500, whichever is less. If you are covered by more than one retirement plan, your total voluntary contributions may not exceed $2,500 per year. While you may not deduct the additional contribution, you benefit from the tax-free accumulation of earnings in the fund.

Savings Payout Plans

Many savings banks and savings and loan associations have retirement payout plans for their depositors. Say, because you have a company pension plan, you cannot establish an IRA plan. Though a payout plan at your savings institution is not the same as an IRA since it does not enjoy the same tax-protection features for contributions and build-up of principal, it can enable you to receive regular checks during your retirement years and still leave money to your beneficiaries after your death. Your monthly checks are tax free although you must continue to pay tax on the interest as earned.

Based on an interest rate of 5.47 percent effective annual yield, here are some examples of a savings payout plan:

At age 45, you deposit $20 a month for twenty years, giving you a total of $8,585 (including interest). At age 65 for 10 years you can receive $92 a month, a total payout of $11,112. If you wanted to leave that original $8,585 to a beneficiary, you could choose to receive monthly for the rest of your life (not just 10 years), the sum of $38.15 without depleting the principal.

Now say you put $100 a month into the account between the ages of 45 and 65. With dividends, you have accumulated $42,926 which could be paid out to you for a 20-year period at a rate of

$291 a month, a total of $69,949. Or, by taking only $190.78 each month for the rest of your life, the original $42,926 is still on hand for your beneficiaries.

If you could save as much as $416 a month you have $178,572 with dividends in twenty years, when you could draw $1,211 a month for 20 years, receiving a total of $209,909. Or, take only $793.68 for the rest of your life and leave $178,572 to beneficiaries.

The actual figures in your case might be very different since you might save at new and higher rates, and might start at an earlier age or later in life. Generally, you would convert your regular savings account to a payout plan near retirement time. You might decide to put several bank accounts into one savings institution which had a payout plan. Say you placed $10,000 in a new account. You could start drawing $100 a month for the next 11 years and receive a total of $13,253, or take only $44.44 a month for life and leave the original $10,000 to beneficiaries. Larger and smaller amounts work the same way, so nearing retirement, you might wish to liquidate assets that might prove troublesome or risky and establish a payout savings plan with your capital.

With this type of plan, of course, you can start at any age you please. Also, savings institutions will pay out dividends each quarter if that income will meet your needs.

Remember these points: savings bank interest is subject to ordinary income tax rates, both Federal and state; and the quoted amounts represent fixed-dollars. The $100 a month placed in a savings account monthly over the years is of decreasing value if the economy is inflationary. But savings accounts are safe and predictable investments; they are currently insured for $40,000 by the FDIC or FSLIC. This amount may be revised upwards by the regulatory agencies.

Real Estate Investments

The specialized field of real estate has proven highly profitable to investors who study its cycles and move in at the right time. Too, alert couples have developed a personal business by buying homes, furnishing them tastefully, living in them a time, and then selling, complete to the last picture on the wall. Others derive a useful income from seasonal renting of a second home in a summer or winter resort area. You may be one of those who can profitably invest in real estate. But there are many pitfalls. You may know of senior citizens who have been deceived by glib advertising of swamp or desert areas as "Your Retirement Home in Paradise" or "Profitable Real Estate Investment."

Though older people are by no means the only ones victimized by land fraud, the fact that many retirees are free to go to a changed climate, have money to put into a new home, and are often unsophisticated in real estate deals makes this class of citizen a prime target for rackets. Though you may be a well-educated professional or business person, buying lots for a home or as an investment may be outside your previous experience. Before getting into any deals, check on the developer and the property with the Department of Housing and Urban Development's Interstate Land Sales Registration office (Washington D.C. 20410, or in your area). A development may be Federally registered but that is no guarantee it is on the level.

You may not realize that even fine property desirably located can result in years of anxiety and financial loss which can be particularly burdensome to the older person. Take the case of Martha Jay, a well-to-do widow, who owned a home in Connecticut. In the late 1950's, she bought two houses in Florida, one for winter living, the other for renting. Soon she ran into renting difficulties; some tenants were destructive; some failed to pay rent. Mrs. Jay put the rental property up for sale. Though excellently situated, the house dragged on the market, the victim of hurricanes, vandals, and, occasionally, its tenants. Continually, the owner drew on her resources to support it. When she tried to sell the other Florida home, it too stuck on the market.

The property-entangled widow tried two options: selling both Florida properties and renting vacation living quarters; selling the Connecticut home so she could move into one of the Florida homes. Neither worked. Despite the genuine value of the three properties, the right buyers did not appear. The widow, burdened by increasing years and ill-health, had to continue to spend money where she had hoped to receive income.

Though another person approaching retirement age might not experience the same misfortunes as Mrs. Jay, especially in a flourishing real estate market, the warning is plain; avoid tying up capital in investments that lack liquidity and immediate marketability; avoid investments that require the personal attention which becomes burdensome to older people. (True, an agent will handle real estate problems, but his services will add to the cost of unprofitable ventures.)

On the other hand, you may already have enjoyed success in real estate investment. With knowledge of the field, you can count on income from sales and rentals in your retirement years. Others who, like Mrs. Jay, have no more experience in real estate than home ownership, should be wary in their later years of channeling all their money into investment property.

CHAPTER 8

Keeping Records to Reduce Taxes

Income taxes are inevitable, and for most taxpayers, a very heavy annual expense. Year after year, they cut deeply into income. But you can take the steps necessary to reduce your taxes and in this chapter you will find one necessary approach to income tax savings, that is keeping records. Record keeping is an essential part of your all-around tax planning. Your detailed records will help you figure your income and deductions at the end of the year. Do not trust to memory. With bills accumulating during a year, you are bound to overlook items. But more important, you will have no record to present to the IRS if they should call you down.

Make a rule to keep a detailed record of any expense ordinary and necessary to the production of income. Keep bills for investment, legal, or tax counsel, or for rent of a safe deposit box. Legal or accounting fees paid for advice on investments are tax deductible. Also deductible are costs involved in the preparation of a tax return.

When you hold property as an investment, keep statements of expenses pertaining to maintenance, management, or conservation of the property. You may deduct these even if there is no probability that the property ever will be sold at a gain or produce income. Included in such expenses are: (1) Investment counsel fees or commissions. (2) Custodian fees paid to banks or others. (3)

Auditors' and accountants' fees. (4) Traveling costs for trips away from home to look after investments, conferring with your attorney, accountant, trustee, or investment counsel about tax or income problems. (5) Maintenance costs of idle property where effort has been made to rent or sell.

Good record keeping applies particularly to rental property. Because there are many deductible expenses involved, record keeping is extremely important. You must have a complete record of the cost of the property, including legal fees, title insurance, the date the property was acquired, the date and cost of each material alteration or addition. The records you must keep during each year include:

1. Amount of rental income received.
2. Bills paid for utilities (heat, light, water, gas, telephone).
3. Bills paid for repairs (painting, cleaning, papering, redecoration).
4. Property taxes.
5. Management expenses.
6. Salaries and wages paid to janitors, elevator men, service men, maintenance men, etc. and Social Security taxes paid on their wages.
7. Legal expense for drawing short-term leases, dispossessing tenants, acquiring rentals.
8. Fire, liability, plate-glass insurance premiums.
9. Interest on mortgage or other indebtedness.

That you rent only one-half of your house, or one room out of eight, does not change the need for a record of every item. In renting part of your house, you may deduct a proportionate part of the expense of running the house against the rental income. You do not know what to deduct unless you have a record of all the expenses. On the same statement, you can keep an explanation of the basis of the apportionment you use for the tax return.

Even if you occupy the house you own and do not rent any part of it, you are entitled to certain of the deductions listed above. You should keep a record of taxes, interest, and casualty losses for your tax deduction list.

Cancelled checks are adequate proof of contributions you make, which are deductible. But contributions may be in forms other than cash. Keep a record, therefore, of the cost of articles you purchase and give to charitable or religious organizations. This may include such items as donations of food baskets, contributions to bazaars, preparation of food for charitable dinners or picnics. Or if you give household or miscellaneous articles to recognized charitable, religious, educational, or similar organizations (such as Red Cross or a hospital) establish a fair-market value of the property you give and keep a list of the contributions.

If your work involves travel, you should keep a day-by-day record of expenses.

If you have purchased appliances, an auto or other goods or services on the installment plan, keep a record of the interest portion of your payments.

For dividend and interest income from stocks and bonds or for trading investments, keep a record of: (1) Name of issuing company. (2) Number of shares or bonds owned and certificate or serial number of each. (3) Date of purchase. (4) Amount paid (including stamp taxes and broker's fees). (5) Date of sale. (6) Amount received (net after stamp taxes and broker's fees). (7) Broker's statements. (8) Each dividend or interest payment received.

You may hold a number of shares of stock of the same company purchased at different times at varying prices. If you wish to sell some of them the question of whether you have a gain or a loss and whether short-term or long-term depends on which particular securities you sell. If you cannot identify each particular lot and its cost, the law will assume that the shares you are selling are those you first acquired. This may be contrary to what you really wish. Consider the case of an investor who didn't bother to keep the certificate numbers of the various shares he bought from time to time. When he sold some of the stock in a declining market, he thought he was selling shares he had bought at a high price and was therefore taking a tax loss, but when an agent of the Internal Revenue Service questioned the deduction, he couldn't prove which shares he had sold; he didn't have any records. The result was that the agent ruled he had sold shares that had been bought cheaply. Instead of taking a tax loss that he needed to offset other income, he realized a taxable gain in a top tax year.

Here are some pointers to help you avoid this trouble:

1. Keep a record of each certificate registered in your name.

The date it was acquired, the certificate number, and any other identification should be recorded. How it was acquired should be shown. Then, when it is sold, you can identify the particular certificate number sold. You need not sell the earliest acquired shares first.

2. If the certificate numbers are unknown, you should inform your broker (and have him confirm) that you wish to sell particular lots. The broker should be told the date of purchase. If possible, the original purchase memorandum should be referred to, giving date and number.

3. If the certificates were received as a stock dividend or in the exercise of rights, the date they were issued should be recorded. The date the option was exercised, the numbers, and other information should be noted. When a sale is ordered, this date should be referred to precisely and the dealer given the facts.

4. When new certificates for old are received in a recapitalization or in a reorganization, each particular certificate should be identified with the old certificate. This is done by taking the lowest numbered certificate of the new and identifying it with the lowest numbered certificate of the old. Then the next higher numbers are correlated. When finished, all the new certificates should be correlated with the old certificate numbers.

5. All brokers' and dealers' purchase and sales memoranda should be kept, together with all notices or slips from the corporation whose securities are held.

Your records should be kept for a minimum of three years after the year to which they are applicable. Some authorities advise keeping them for six years, since in some cases the IRS may go back as far as six years to question a tax return. In cases of suspected tax fraud, there is no time limitation at all.

Check Record Book

If you wish to keep a combined record of your checking account and tax deductions, you may be interested in J.K. Lasser's Check-Record Book, a page of which is reproduced, greatly reduced,

record of deposits

record of

Date	Source of Items Deposited	Amount of Each Deposit Item		Amount of Total Deposit		Amount		Check No.	Date	To Whom Paid	Explanation
	Opening Balance			$		$					
		$									
*1	TOTAL OF OPENING BALANCE PLUS DEPOSITS										
2	LESS: TOTAL EXPENDITURES									BANK CHARGES	
3	BALANCE CARRIED FORWARD					$				TOTAL MONTHLY EXPENDITURES	

checks you draw

DEDUCTIBLE EXPENSES

month of _____

Taxes	Interest	Medical & Drugs	Contri-butions	Other: Job Costs Tax Help, etc.	Insurance	Savings & Invest.	Home: Utilities, Repairs, etc.	Personal: Food, Clothing, etc.	Auto & Trans-portation
$	$	$	$	$	$	$	$	$	$
$	$	$	$	$	$	$	$	$	$

Note: For tax purposes — mark plainly any business expenditures for transportation, entertainment, etc.

on p. 158-159. The actual book is 8½" x 11" and is therefore large enough for you to fill in the necessary information. Summary forms are also provided so that you have, at year's end, an immediate, complete record of your deductible expenses already broken down for entry on your tax return. Keeping this type of record throughout the year is no more trouble than maintaining your usual accounting of checks while at the same time you note your tax-deductible expenses and so lighten the burden which falls each April.

To obtain a copy of the Check-Record Book, follow the instructions on the last page of this book.

J. K. Lasser's CHECK RECORD BOOK is a slim, compact paperback that replaces your checkbook and helps you to manage your cash for budgeting and tax purposes. It provides you with the records of your receipts and disbursements during the year and serves as an automatic and accurate record of the financial information you need at tax time.

To order the CHECK RECORD BOOK, send your check or money order for $2.50 each (plus sales tax, if applicable) to:

BUSINESS REPORTS, INC.
1 West Avenue
Larchmont, N.Y. 10538

A full refund is available if you are not satisfied with the CHECK RECORD BOOK.